Migrating ASP.NET Microservices to ASP.NET Core 8

Second Edition

Iris Classon

Migrating ASP.NET Microservices to ASP.NET Core 8, Second Edition

Iris Classon
29 Gothenburg, Sweden

ISBN-13 (pbk): 979-8-8688-1025-1   ISBN-13 (electronic): 979-8-8688-1026-8
https://doi.org/10.1007/979-8-8688-1026-8

Managing Director, Apress Media LLC: Welmoed Spahr
Acquisitions Editor: Ryan Byrnes
Development Editor: Laura Berendson
Coordinating Editor: Gryffin Winkler

Cover designed by eStudioCalamar

Cover image designed by Freepik (www.freepik.com)

Distributed to the book trade worldwide by Apress Media, LLC, 1 New York Plaza, New York, NY 10004, U.S.A. Phone 1-800-SPRINGER, fax (201) 348-4505, e-mail orders-ny@springer-sbm.com, or visit www.springeronline.com. Apress Media, LLC is a California LLC and the sole member (owner) is Springer Science + Business Media Finance Inc (SSBM Finance Inc). SSBM Finance Inc is a **Delaware** corporation.

For information on translations, please e-mail booktranslations@springernature.com; for reprint, paperback, or audio rights, please e-mail bookpermissions@springernature.com.

Apress titles may be purchased in bulk for academic, corporate, or promotional use. eBook versions and licenses are also available for most titles. For more information, reference our Print and eBook Bulk Sales web page at http://www.apress.com/bulk-sales.

Any source code or other supplementary material referenced by the author in this book is available to readers on GitHub (https://github.com/Apress). For more detailed information, please visit https://www.apress.com/gp/services/source-code.

If disposing of this product, please recycle the paper

To my husband, for your unwavering support and belief in my writing.

To my two boys, for finally sleeping through the night (most nights) and allowing me the quiet moments to create.

To the .NET developer community, who has always welcomed me with open arms, fueling my passion and inspiring me every step of the way.

And to the exceptional team at Apress, it's a privilege to work with you.

Table of Contents

About the Author

 **Iris Classon** is a force of nature. Her unique and engaging methods of teaching complex topics have garnered her considerable respect from the developer community and significant media attention – Channel 9, Hanselminutes, Computer Sweden, and Developer Magazine, to name a few. A Microsoft MVP with multiple certifications, Iris is currently an app developer at Plejd, a leading Nordic supplier of smart lighting solutions.

Iris is also a prolific author, having written over a dozen books. She continues to inspire and educate through her popular blog, YouTube videos, and social media channels, including X (formerly known as Twitter) (@IrisClasson). A frequent speaker at conferences such as TechDays and NDC, Iris is deeply committed to sharing knowledge with the global developer community.

About the Technical Reviewer

**Amol Gote** is an accomplished Solutions Architect with over two decades of experience designing and developing scalable, resilient microservices for FinTech and enterprises. He has built microservices using both .NET and Java. He specializes in cloud-based software development and has led several innovative projects with FinTech and large financial organizations and enterprises. He has spent seven years with Microsoft in the early part of his career. He excels in deploying and managing microservices in AWS and Azure environments, boasting technical proficiency across multiple applications and tools. His expertise spans full-stack capabilities, from designing to constructing end-to-end solutions that include databases (SQL/NoSQL), back-end services, messaging services, and modern interactive web applications using web sockets.

IIis work often focuses on creating secure, user-friendly platforms that provide accessible financial solutions. He also contributes to open source projects and has authored research papers and articles in financial technology, cloud computing, and microservices. Amol is passionate about writing blogs and technical articles for online platforms like DZone. He has also served as a judge and mentor at various events. Amol's commitment to excellence is evident in his multiple certifications, including AWS Certified Solutions Architect and various Microsoft certifications. Amol holds numerous awards for his contributions to the FinTech field.

Introduction

I still vividly remember the thrill of discovering new programming languages and tools after graduating. Despite years of experience and a more cynical view of ever-changing frameworks, I remain passionate about technology. When .NET Core was announced, my initial reaction was skepticism mixed with curiosity – like my early days experimenting with Portable Class Libraries. However, I knew that jumping straight into ASP. NET Core without solid evidence of its benefits was premature.

As adoption of ASP.NET Core grew and it showed clear advantages in handling legacy issues, my workplace began considering its potential for our projects. Yet, the lack of comprehensive, up-to-date information on migrating large systems was a significant barrier. This book aims to fill that gap. It will not serve as an exhaustive guide on ASP.NET Core itself – there are many excellent resources for that – but will focus on migration strategies:

- Analysis and inventory
- Planning and preparation
- Step-by-step migration process
- Deployment pipeline and maintenance post-migration

This guide includes practical examples from a complex system, detailed steps for migration, and an extensive list of resources and tools. I hope it provides all the information I initially struggled to find, helping you make informed decisions and focus on creating great software with ASP. NET Core.

Laying the Groundwork

When I first outlined this book, my plan was to assume that you, the reader, had a basic understanding of ASP.NET Core, allowing us to dive straight into the migration process. However, I recognize that as developers, we often face time constraints that delay our deep dives into new technologies. Therefore, at the start of this book, I will take a moment to share my insights and highlight some key features of ASP.NET Core that you might not yet know about.

This foundational knowledge is crucial not only for a smoother migration but also for ensuring a comprehensive understanding of the broader .NET ecosystem.

CHAPTER 1

The Evolution of ASP.NET Core

Let's take a brief journey through the history of ASP.NET Core. If you've been in the field for some time, you might remember the days of Classic ASP (Active Server Pages) in the early 1990s, which marked a significant advancement in dynamically rendering server-side pages with integrated logic. This evolved into ASP 1.0 and later transformed into ASP.NET with Web Forms in 2001, offering a more structured framework for web development.

By 2009, ASP.NET MVC was introduced as a necessary alternative to Web Forms, aligning with the industry's shift toward separation of concerns and testability in web applications. Alongside these developments, communication technologies progressed from early methods like DDE (Dynamic Data Exchange) and DCOM to more sophisticated frameworks like .NET Remoting and ASP Web Services, culminating in the release of WCF (Windows Communication Foundation) in 2006. WCF aimed to unify these diverse communication methods under a single service-oriented framework.

© Iris Classon 2024
I. Classon, *Migrating ASP.NET Microservices to ASP.NET Core 8*,
https://doi.org/10.1007/979-8-8688-1026-8_1

Despite its broad capabilities, WCF struggled with REST support, leading to the development of the WCF Web API project. This project eventually evolved into Web API, which resonated well with the ASP.NET MVC programming model because of its flexibility and ease of use. When ASP.NET Core was developed as a complete rewrite of ASP.NET, it naturally integrated features from both Web API and MVC.

As web development continued to evolve, the need for a more unified and modern approach became clear, paving the way for ASP.NET Core – a complete rewrite designed to meet the demands of today's complex, cross-platform applications.

Core and More

There were two major driving forces that led to what we today know as .NET, formerly .NET Core. First, there was an increasing need for cross-platform compatibility to stay relevant, and second, we had gotten to a place where we had too many subsets of the .NET Framework, which was causing many problems as the subsets were created and maintained by different teams. 2014 was the year Microsoft made many exciting announcements. ASP.NET vNext was announced in April, and .NET Core in November the same year. .NET Core was a fork and open source rewrite of .NET, and likewise ASP.NET vNext was a complete rewrite of ASP.NET. It was later known as ASP.NET 5 (and by some as project K) until Microsoft realized the name was confusing and renamed it to ASP.NET Core.

Around the time .NET Standard was launched, its aim was to create a unified set of APIs that all .NET implementations would follow, ensuring that code could seamlessly operate across different .NET environments. However, introducing .NET 5 – essentially a rebranded .NET Core – marked a shift toward a singular, integrated .NET platform for all future development, achieving what had always been the goal. ASP.NET Core Blazor, alongside MAUI, further emphasized this shift toward a more unified and versatile

development ecosystem. Blazor is a front-end web framework within the
.NET ecosystem that facilitates both server-side rendering and client-side
interactivity using a unified programming model, and .NET MAUI, which
stands for .NET Multi-platform App UI, is a cross-platform framework
designed for building native mobile and desktop applications using C#
and XAML.

The journey of .NET Framework reached a turning point with version 4.8,
marking the culmination of the "traditional" .NET era, with .NET 5 continuing
the path as an updated .NET Core.

While .NET Standard libraries remain supported for compatibility with
this unified .NET, developers are now encouraged to focus on the latest
.NET versions for new projects. As of the latest updates, the latest .NET
versions are now being encouraged for new projects. NET Framework 4.8
is still supported. However, the .NET Framework 4.6.1, which is used in the
system we discuss in this book, reached its end of life in 2022. Eventually,
.NET Framework 4.8 will follow suit.

To sum up, ASP.NET Core is the next step in the web development
evolution, an evolution that goes back over 30 years. During that time, a lot
has happened; tools and frameworks have been developed and matured.
The goal has always been to make it easier for us as developers to create
performant, flexible, yet sturdy services that allow freedom in terms of
how we communicate over the network and serve our content. ASP.NET
Core brings together the best bits from other frameworks and gives us the
flexibility to pick the operating system that fits our needs perfectly. It's all
about boosting performance and encouraging best practices, making it a
go-to for building modern web applications. For now, ASP.NET Core is the
future of web development with the Microsoft stack.

Benefits of Migrating

Here is a summarized overview of what many consider as the main benefits of migrating to ASP.NET Core. For a comprehensive list, please visit https://learn.microsoft.com/aspnet/core.

Latest Language and API Features

Staying up to date and being able to access the latest language and API features was particularly important for us so we could improve our codebase, write better and cleaner code, and be able to update dependencies to the latest versions. As an example, Minimal APIs, which we will discuss in-depth later, was one of the new API features we were particularly interested in, as well as gRPC support.

Performance

Due to the nature of the application, performance was the most important win for us as we have a system that does heavy work, a lot of calculations, and would also need to be able to handle many concurrent requests. With the .NET 6 release performance had improved by more than 80%, and subsequent releases have further improved performance. In a .NET7 performance blog post, Microsoft shared the following impressive benchmarks: plaintext platform benchmark improved by 514%, 2.4m RPS to 14.6m RPS. As for JSON, a 311% improvement, and 270k RPS to 1.1m RPS. To put this into perspective, these improvements mean faster response times and more efficient use of server resources, which translates to reduced latency for end users and the ability to handle more traffic without additional infrastructure. For example, if your application previously required five Azure D2s_v3 VMs to handle its load, the enhanced efficiency of .NET 7 could theoretically reduce that to just two VMs. In practice, however, factors like redundancy, backups, and elastic scaling options would also need to be considered.

It's important to remember that ASP.NET Core was a complete rewrite, which means it could be written with performance in mind. But many things contributed to the remarkable speed. Smaller apps, clever allocations, better management of the thread pool and sockets, vectorized HTTP parser, and more. Performance work is tagged as such in the GitHub repository if you'd like to keep an eye on specific changes in that area.

If you want to learn more about the benchmarking, visit the repository at `https://github.com/aspnet/benchmarks`.

Built-in Dependency Injection and Logging

In the redesign of ASP.NET Core, Microsoft, together with the developer community, aimed to embed best practices from the outset while significantly improving the framework. Two notable advancements include the integration of built-in dependency injection (DI) and enhanced logging capabilities. For those already familiar with DI, ASP.NET Core's approach may not seem revolutionary, but its ability to seamlessly incorporate various container resolvers stands out. This integration ensures that everything functions smoothly once set up.

Dependency injection in ASP.NET Core is designed to naturally fit within the framework's ecosystem. For instance, the handling of configuration files also leverages DI, utilizing the Options pattern. This allows developers to map configuration sections directly to classes implementing the "IOptions<T>" interface, facilitating strongly typed access to settings. This seamless integration of DI exemplifies how ASP.NET Core promotes improved software practices.

Dependency injection is a technique where you map a concrete type to an abstraction, such as an interface, and inject that interface into the constructor of another class, rather than creating a new concrete instance within that class. The abstraction and implementation are typically mapped and resolved from a DI container. This promotes loose coupling, simplifies testing and mocking, and allows for various ways to resolve dependencies – whether as singletons, per request, or per resolution.

The IOptions<T> pattern in ASP.NET Core exemplifies the advantages of DI. Instead of directly accessing configuration settings within your classes, you can inject an IOptions<T> instance. This instance encapsulates the settings, making them easier to manage and change without modifying dependent classes. This approach simplifies testing and mocking while promoting a more modular and maintainable codebase. For instance, when running the solution locally, you can inject local settings via environment variables, config files, or command-line arguments, and then seamlessly swap these out for stage or production settings in other environments. This ensures sensitive information isn't hardcoded and avoids the complexity of managing multiple configuration providers. Additionally, when testing, you can easily mock the settings, allowing you to test various scenarios without needing to rely on an actual configuration provider.

As you can see, by adopting these enhanced practices, ASP.NET Core encourages flexible and maintainable code. This is particularly beneficial for systems that frequently undergo modifications, such as Konstrukt, helping to avoid the pitfalls of rigid solutions.

Modularity

One thing I didn't mention in the preceding section is the modular HTTP request pipeline, a result of implementing the OWIN specification. This is available in ASP.NET with Katana, but comes more naturally in ASP.NET Core. To explain this in simple terms, you can very easily plug in your own middleware that interacts with the requests and responses on their way in and out. We use this to modify our requests, custom logging, and a few more things. It lets us return or redirect early in the request processing.

This modularity is a theme that you see throughout ASP.NET Core. For example, everything is a NuGet package. You don't add references, you add NuGet packages. And there are many packages, because the big ASP. NET Framework has been completely rewritten in ASP.NET Core to consist of many smaller libraries. The upside is that Microsoft can release more often; the downside is of course version alignment and dependencies.

This has been sorted with metapackages, a package that references other packages. It includes all supported packages by the ASP.NET Core team and the Entity Framework team. We'll talk more about this later.

Perfect for Containers

By nature, .NET Core is lightweight and modular, which makes it much easier to use with containers. Container is the concept of virtualization at the operating system level. From the inside of a container, it is a self-contained machine. It thinks it has its own operating system and everything that comes with it. For the services running inside the container (virtual boundaries), it feels like they run on a dedicated machine. In reality, they share the same machine as other containers using the same host and can only access resources within the container or explicitly made available. It feels like a virtual machine, but you don't have the overhead of a guest operating system, startup time, and more. The operating system is reused, and instead virtual boundaries let us work with containers as if they were separate machines. You basically bundle your application with everything it needs, and you get consistency, portability, flexibility, testability, and isolation in one package.

Containers have been around for a long time in the Linux world, but security and isolation concerns impeded the container movement on Windows. Thankfully we have seen massive changes the last few years, and now containers are first-class citizen even on Windows and in Visual Studio. As a matter of fact, you can run your applications in containers straight from the IDE.

Open Source and Community Driven

I mentioned earlier that ASP.NET Core is open source, and this is fantastic. There are many good things that come with that, and transparency is the biggest one I would say. I can see the roadmap and join in on the discussion if I want to; I can see issues and breaking changes, suggestions, and discussions. And an active community is doing the same and keeps pushing the projects forward all while making sure that best practices are followed and possible future issues are considered.

Cross-Platform Support

ASP.NET Core allows developers to build and run applications on multiple platforms, including Windows, Linux, and macOS. This flexibility facilitates a broader reach and makes it easier to manage development environments across different systems. In theory, we can have lighter containers – and a host that doesn't necessarily require a license. As a result, we can increase the concurrent services density.

Moreover, this allows us to expand our isolated testing environment to several environments such as Quality Assurance (QA) and Acceptance Testing (AT) without the cost or hardware overhead. However, if you can't target the .NET Core framework and you have some services that have to target the full .NET Framework, you can still benefit from both containers and the cross-platform ability. Something called "hybrid swarm" (a swarm is a cluster of containers) lets us run mixed environment containers – in other words, we can run Windows and Linux applications in one cluster.

As a startup, cost has been an issue for us straight from the start and also has been something that hindered our deployment pipeline as we have crammed several services on one machine to save money. With better isolation comes easier scaling, debugging, and deploying.

Besides these, there are also other benefits to running on other platforms – and for us that is the access to mature and well-maintained tools. While most Linux tools have a Windows equivalent, there are still some tools that have a higher maturity level on Linux that we would love to leverage.

The Downside

The biggest downside of migrating is by far the cost, which unfortunately is hard to estimate. While you can guard yourself by scrutinizing the documentation and look for specific breaking changes that might require more work, it's impossible to say exactly how much work is required to migrate. This book should help with that, and with proper planning, the migration should go smoother and take less time.

Summary

We've covered a lot of ground in this chapter, tracing the evolution of ASP.NET into the robust framework that is ASP.NET Core today. From its enhanced performance and modularity, to best-practices design patterns and cross-platform versatility, ASP.NET Core is built to meet the demands of modern web development. As we continue through this book, we'll dive into the migration process, exploring the tools and techniques that will help you transition to ASP.NET Core smoothly. But before we get into that, let's take a closer look at Konstrukt, the SaaS solution we're migrating in this book.

CHAPTER 2

Case in Study: Konstrukt SaaS System

When I first began working with Konstrukt, I didn't expect it would lead me into the startup world. What started as a one-off favor for a friend turned into late-night coding sessions, all driven by the need to fix some persistent performance issues and bugs. The caffeine-fueled weekends quickly became the norm as we worked out of a small office overlooking the city center.

The original system was designed for just two local clients, but as the client list grew, so did the need to scale. This prompted a shift to a cloud-based, multitenant solution using Azure, requiring significant code rewrites alongside promised feature updates and bug fixes. It became clear that migrating to ASP.NET Core wasn't just a technical upgrade but a strategic pivot to address our growing pains.

In this chapter, I'll take you through the functionality and architecture of Konstrukt, the SaaS platform we're migrating. This includes a look at its components, the challenges we faced, and the solutions we implemented. By sharing real code snippets – anonymized for confidentiality – I aim to provide a realistic scenario that you can relate to as you embark on your own projects.

© Iris Classon 2024
I. Classon, *Migrating ASP.NET Microservices to ASP.NET Core 8*,
https://doi.org/10.1007/979-8-8688-1026-8_2

Installation Requirements

While ASP.NET Core supports running on Linux and can be used with editors like Visual Studio Code, for this project, I've opted to use Visual Studio on Windows. This choice is primarily because of the additional tools and extensions available on this platform that simplify the migration process. However, it's important to note that these tools are conveniences, not necessities. The core steps of the migration process do not rely on these specific tools, and I will also discuss alternative methods throughout this book to ensure flexibility regardless of your development environment.

Requirements for a migration using the steps described in the book:

- Windows (latest version)

- Visual Studio (latest version)

- .NET Core SDK (latest or the version you are targeting) Additional requirements for running the examples in the book:

- IIS 7 or later

- Git and Git Bash

- SQL Server Express 2016 or later

- Postman

Multitenant Software as a Service (SaaS)

The system itself is, as mentioned earlier, a multitenant solution. It's a SaaS system (Software as a Service), which means it has a cloud computing service model with a centrally hosted system. The clients, whom we refer to as tenants, do not have to manage or control the infrastructure.

That is unless they choose, or rather insist on, an on-premises installation. Most clients prefer the SaaS solution, however, there are exceptions, such as certain government institutions that, because of legal constraints, require on an on-premises installation. Despite these outliers, the beauty of our multitenancy approach is that it appears to each tenant as if they have their own dedicated cloud installation. In reality, they all share the same applications and services. This setup significantly reduces our burden of managing multiple infrastructure setups, streamlining operations and maintenance across the board.

We get the benefit of not having to manage x-number of infrastructure setups and discuss hardware and software requirements and licenses, support becomes more manageable, and we can roll out patches and updates as we please. There is also a significant financial gain to this, which is another important factor. While our system offers numerous benefits, it also presents several significant challenges. Leading among these are data security and maintaining consistent uptime – both critical to fulfilling our Service Level Agreements (SLAs) with our tenants. Additionally, we must adhere to SLAs established with our cloud vendor and the various services we utilize there.

A particularly complex challenge we face, common to many SaaS solutions, involves managing load, latency, and overall performance. The nature of load in a cloud-based environment is inherently unpredictable, which complicates capacity planning and resource allocation. Furthermore, the performance issues that were already present in our on-premise solutions have intensified since our transition to the cloud. This is primarily because our application handles large volumes of data, which can exacerbate latency and load problems as the system scales.

What the System Does

Konstrukt is a versatile planning platform designed for a variety of organizations to manage diverse data-driven planning and budgeting. It efficiently handles everything from simple quantitative planning and data consolidation to more complex scenarios, all in a secure and user-friendly environment. This flexibility makes it an ideal replacement for the widespread misuse of Excel in many organizational settings.

The platform supports a broad spectrum of planning needs, including strategic planning, rolling forecasting, data-driven budgeting, workforce capacity planning, compensation, and equity planning. One of the persistent challenges we face is maintaining optimal performance, a topic I will delve into in the next chapter as we weigh the pros and cons of undergoing a migration.

Architecture

Konstrukt is built on a convoluted structure comprising nine ASP.NET Web API services, alongside a stateless and decoupled client developed using JavaScript, HTML, and CSS. As illustrated in Figure 2-1, each tenant operates their own database, with our platform currently utilizing SQL Server exclusively. Although most services access shared databases on the same server cluster – sometimes differentiated only by schemas – we also incorporate NoSQL databases like MongoDB for certain services.

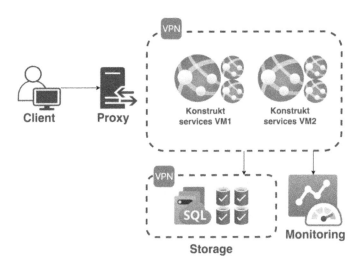

Figure 2-1. *The system we are migrating*

At first glance, this setup might suggest a microservice architecture due to the distribution of services. However, despite the presence of multiple services, Konstrukt functions more like a distributed monolith. This means that while the system might appear to be a collection of small, independent services, they are heavily reliant on shared data stores and lack individual failure resistance – traits that are typically not characteristic of a true microservice architecture.

This situation often leads to a debate among developers about what truly defines microservices. For the purpose of this book, which discusses migrating microservices, it's important to note that we will be dealing with services that vary in their level of decoupling and failure resistance. This approach will provide a realistic view of the challenges and strategies involved in migrating complex systems, whether they are considered legacy or not.

If your system is a monolith – or a single-tier application – there's no need for concern. Some of our services also lean toward monolithic architecture, and this book addresses these scenarios as well.

As we dive into the migration process, I'll be using a few of our services as examples to illustrate the steps and strategies involved. To give you a clearer picture of our entire system and how these services interact, here's a brief overview of the main services and their specific functions.

Authentication

Manages authentication. We support several authentication methods, such as

- Internal database login

- ADFS

- SAML2

- And a few more

After the initial authentication, a JWT (JSON Web Token) is provided as an authentication header. This token is saved on the client and used for subsequent requests.

Administration

Manages all the logic that is available for system admins, such as setting access rights and importing users.

Main

This service is mainly concerned with actions that are driven by actions in the client. Two examples would be when a user sends in a budget for approval and when a user adds a comment on a budget.

AggregationEngine

Writes and reads budget data to the user budget line tables.

CalculationEngine

Queues and processes calculations that generate data for the different plans and budgets.

ReportingService

Generates Excel reports and PNG graphs by using a GAC (Global Assembly Cache) library for budget predictions.

NotificationService

Manages notifications, currently WebSocket notifications. Notifications can be messages in the chat or user notifications when a budget has been submitted for approval. We use SignalR for our notifications, a popular library for working with real-time web communication.

As you probably have concluded, the system is of considerable size. It's not colossal, but large nonetheless. For the purpose of this book, I've trimmed the solution, and I have some particular services in mind that will receive more attention in this book, as shown in Figure 2-2.

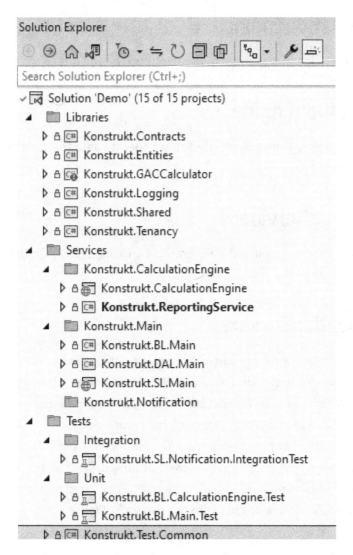

Figure 2-2. *The trimmed down version of Konstrukt that I'm using in this book*

This book zeroes in on the migration of Konstrukt.SL.Main and Konstrukt. CalculationEngine, along with their interrelated components as depicted in Figure 2-3. We'll also explore the strategic use of .NET Standard for shared dependencies associated with services that we won't be migrating immediately.

Konstrukt.SL.Main serves as the original module of our platform and, over time, has inevitably become entangled with what one might affectionately call "spaghetti code." Embracing a microservices architecture prompted us to delineate and delegate specific functionalities to distinct services, making Konstrukt.SL.Main a prime candidate for decomposition. I will delve deeper into this transition and its intricacies later in the book.

I also want to mention the notification service, which manages WebSocket notifications using SignalR. This is a lightweight service with just a few dependencies that are popular libraries, which makes it a good candidate for a full migration. We use SignalR to send real-time notifications to users whenever a budget is changed, ensuring that everyone currently working on the project is instantly informed. It also provides updates when calculations are running, notifying users of any issues or when the process has been completed.

ASP.NET Core SignalR differs significantly from the original SignalR, and a migration would require a separate book on the topic. Therefore, I've omitted the code for the service from this discussion.

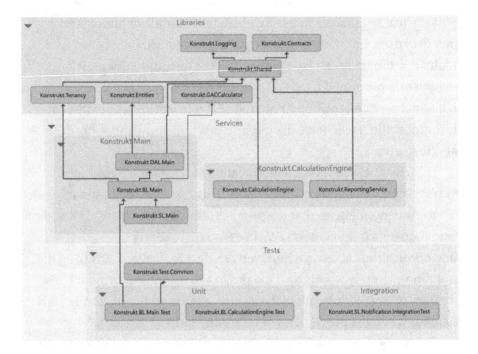

Figure 2-3. *Konstrukt dependency graph*

An extension like ReSharper can be used to generate a dependency diagram for a project. If you don't have a license, you can try ReSharper for free for 30 days. After installing ReSharper, select the project you want to create a dependency diagram for, and select the following options in the main menu: Extensions ➤ ReSharper ➤ Architecture ➤ Show Project Dependency Diagram (Figure 2-4). You can export this diagram as a diagram file (.graphml) or a PNG.

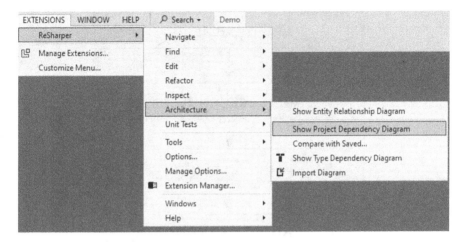

Figure 2-4. *Generating a dependency diagram for a project*

Pipeline

Later in the book, we will also take a look at how we have to modify the pipeline as we migrate our services and libraries.

We use Git as our version control system, and we use GitHub for our repository. We have a build server that runs TeamCity – TeamCity is a build server service. It runs the following build steps sequentially – and if one step fails, the other steps won't run.

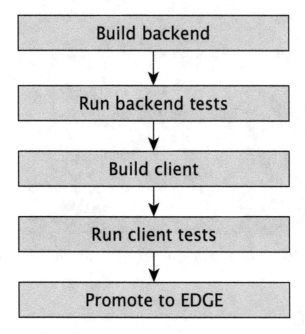

Figure 2-5. *Pipeline flow for Konstrukt*

1. Build back end (builds the back-end code and packages each service as a NuGet package).

2. Run back-end unit tests (runs our unit tests).

3. Build client (builds our client, minifies and bundles resources).

4. Run client tests (runs the client tests in a headless browser).

5. Promote to EDGE (pushes our packages to our EDGE server environment and verifies that all the services can start and run without any issues).

On the build server, we also run a service called Octopus Deploy. Octopus Deploy is an automated release management tool for Windows.

You can automate and manage deployments on remote machines from a central place, and this is done by installing something referred to as "tentacles" on the receiving machines. The tentacles create communication channels that we can push our packages through. The machines are organized in groups tagged as an environment. We have different number of machines depending on the environment. Our EDGE environment is just one virtual machine, because we only want to have a first place to deploy to and make sure everything runs fine. Our second environment is our QA (quality assurance) environment. This is where we do our testing, and we have the services spread out on two machines. Our AT (acceptance testing) environment has four machines and is identical to the production environment, as it is the final stop before deploying to production. Acceptance testing is the final testing that we do, and we have both certain customers and implementation consultants (consultants that help the tenant configure their data and calculations) testing in AT. The final environment, also with four virtual machines, is PROD (production).

Ideally, we would have each service run on a single virtual machine so we would have proper isolation, but unfortunately, that would be too expensive for us. That is also one of the reasons that we would like to migrate our services, and I'm going to talk about that a lot more in the next chapter.

Summary

In this chapter, we've taken a look at the Konstrukt architecture and what the system does. The system consists of nine services, various tools, and a SQL server for storage. Konstrukt does numeric planning for enterprises and manages performance-sensitive operations tied to the planning and data consolidation. Throughout the book, we will use a slice of the system to guide you through a step-by-step migration, including changes to the deployment pipeline.

CHAPTER 3

Analysis and Inventory

It was early summer of 2016, and the team was in Hungary for a week of workshops and fun. Every year we would take a week somewhere remote and spend the days learning new but relevant skills and the afternoons and evenings building a good company culture and exchanging knowledge.

Our team had recently hired another back-end developer, Tobias, and he was just as eager as me to explore .NET Core. We had spent 2 days penetration testing and had finished a security evaluation of the system.

As we sat at a delightful cafe, the conversation shifted to ASP.NET Core and whether it was worth our consideration. Naturally, we began discussing dependencies and what could be migrated – and if we had any deal breakers. I retrieved my laptop and began the process of reviewing our packages and references, one by one.

That was the start of our journey migrating to ASP.NET Core. Although we didn't do a full analysis or even attempt a migration that summer, it created a starting point. We were in the midst of moving to a new cloud provider and had our hands full with the move, but we had explored the pros and cons of migrating, and we had analyzed our solution. No matter what approach you and your team choose, I suggest allocating a few days free from the expectation of delivering outcomes. Adequate preparation will enable you to analyze and streamline the migration process effectively.

I. Classon, *Migrating ASP.NET Microservices to ASP.NET Core 8*,
https://doi.org/10.1007/979-8-8688-1026-8_3

Internal Dependencies Analysis

In this chapter, I will guide you through an analysis using a real-world example (that I have trimmed down for readability). We are going to prepare, analyze, and plan. Let's get started.

Note   If you're using Git for version control, please ensure that you have created a separate branch for the analysis. Alternatively, you can use a copy of the solution to avoid any conflicts. Ideally, you should commit after each significant milestone to have the option of undoing any mistakes if necessary.

Preparing the Projects

When we do an analysis, we want to have as little noise as possible. Furthermore, it is important for us to avoid wasting time on analyzing and planning for dependencies that we are not using. Therefore, we are going to remove unused members, types, and references. Before taking any further action, our first priority will be to upgrade the projects and set a goal to target the latest version of the .NET Framework which is 4.8.

Retargeting

If you don't see the framework version you want to target as an option under Properties ➤ Application ➤ Target Framework, then check for Visual Studio updates, run through them, and then bring up the Visual Studio Installer and make sure that the target framework is installed.

You can retarget by right-clicking a project node in Solution Explorer ➤ Properties ➤ Application. You can change the target framework by selecting the target framework in the Target Framework dropdown as shown in Figure 3-1.

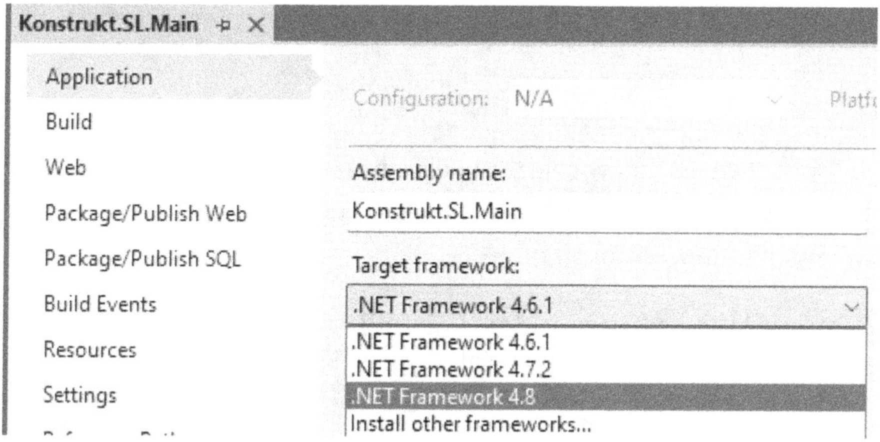

Figure 3-1. *Manually setting a new target framework for a project*

You can also do this by directly editing the .csproj file and changing the TargetFrameWorkVersion in the .csproj file. Depending on the number of projects you have, changing each one can be a significant amount of work. Therefore, I suggest using a script that allows you to retarget all projects simultaneously. Version control lets us undo changes if something goes wrong. Select from the main menu Tools ➤ Command Line ➤ developer PowerShell. The following script will list the projects and the target framework.

```
Get-ChildItem -Recurse -Filter *.csproj | ForEach-Object {
    [xml]$csproj = Get-Content $_.FullName
    $ns = New-Object System.Xml.XmlNamespaceManager($csproj
    .NameTable)
    $ns.AddNamespace("msbuild", "http://schemas.microsoft.com/
    developer/msbuild/2003")
    $targetFrameworkNode = $csproj.SelectSingleNode("//msbuild:
    Project/msbuild:PropertyGroup/msbuild:TargetFramework
    Version", $ns)
    if ($targetFrameworkNode) {
```

```
        "$($_.Name): " + $targetFrameworkNode.InnerText
    }
}
```

Double check that you've pushed to the remote repository, or at least made a copy of the project, before running the following script to update the target framework for all projects.

```
Get-ChildItem -Recurse -Filter *.csproj | ForEach-Object {
    [xml]$csproj = Get-Content $_.FullName
    $ns = New-Object System.Xml.XmlNamespaceManager($csproj
    .NameTable)
    $ns.AddNamespace("msbuild", "http://schemas.microsoft.com/
    developer/msbuild/2003")
    $targetFrameworkNode = $csproj.SelectSingleNode("//msbuild:
    Project/msbuild:PropertyGroup/msbuild:TargetFrameworkVers
    ion", $ns)
    if ($targetFrameworkNode -and $targetFrameworkNode.
    InnerText -ne "v4.8") {
        $targetFrameworkNode.InnerText = "v4.8"
        $csproj.Save($_.FullName)
        Write-Host "Updated $($_.Name) to .NET Framework 4.8"
    } elseif (-not $targetFrameworkNode) {
        Write-Host "No TargetFrameworkVersion found in
        $($_.Name)"
    } else {
        Write-Host "$($_.Name) is already set to .NET
        Framework 4.8"
    }
}
```

If Visual Studio asks you to reload the projects, select Reload All (Figure 3-2).

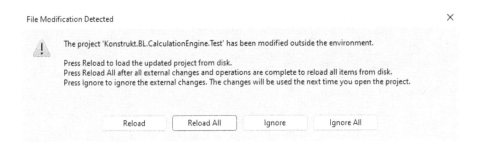

Figure 3-2. *Reload all projects*

Build the solution, verify all the projects, build and run the tests.

Compile and the tests as well, making sure that everything compiles and runs as expected. Our unit tests use NUnit and therefore require the NUnit Test Adapter or ReSharper test runner (Figure 3-3).

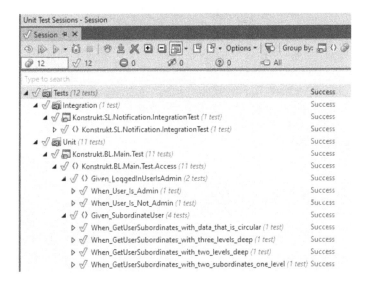

Figure 3-3. *Running the tests in the solution*

If everything checks out, go through the diffs for the changed project files. The Git Changes window, main menu ➤ View ➤ Git Changes will list the changed files (Figure 3-4).

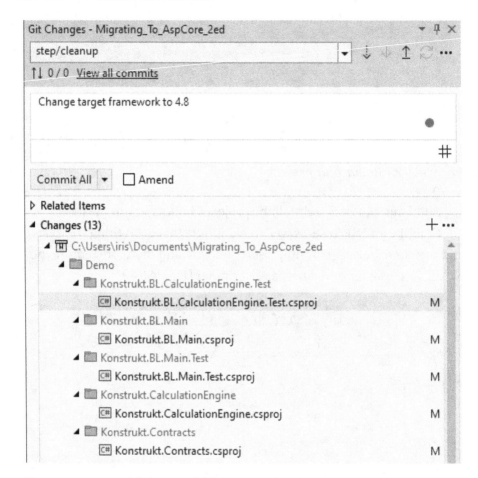

Figure 3-4. *List of changed files*

Make sure only the target framework has been changed (Figure 3-5). Commit the changes.

Figure 3-5. *Only the target framework has been changed*

Our next step is to remove unused types, members, and references. We will continue to use the ReSharper extension for this.

Removing Unused Types and Members

Technically, you don't really have to do this step, but it doesn't take long and can simplify things later. This is something we should do from time to time anyway, and this is a perfect opportunity. With legacy applications and libraries over time, you often end up with types or members that aren't used. These might in turn reference assemblies, and we want to only analyze how much work this migration is going to take based on assemblies, types, and members we are using.

Note   Cleaning up also has the added advantage of improving the maintainability index. The introduction of dependencies frequently results in an increase in complexity.

If you right-click a project (or the solution) and select Analyze ➤ Calculate Code Metrics (Figure 3-6), you will get the project maintainability index as well as other indicators such as cyclomatic dependency, depth of inheritance, class coupling, and lines of code (Figure 3-7).

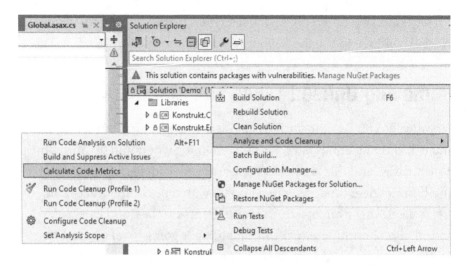

Figure 3-6. *Running a code metrics analysis for a solution*

Figure 3-7. *Code analysis results for Konstrukt*

As a fun add-on for the analysis step, why not go ahead and get the code metrics and export them to Excel. After tidying up the references, you can then run the analysis again and compare the results.

With ReSharper installed and activated, select in the main menu ReSharper ➤ Inspect ➤ Code Issues in Current Project/Solution (select solution if your solution is smaller).

Group by Issue Type and scroll down to "Type member is never used" as shown in Figure 3-8. It shows the result with the filter applied.

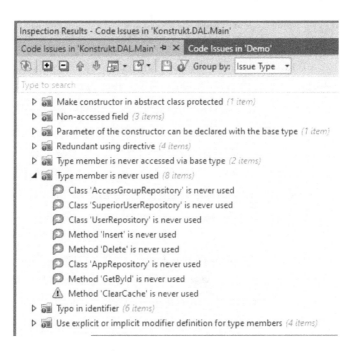

***Figure 3-8.** Code issues for Konstrukt.DAL.Main*

If I navigate to the ClearCache method, ReSharper suggests that I remove the ClearCache method which will remove the method from the interface as well. I can also select to comment out the unused method – I'm personally not a big fan of that, and since we have source control, I'll just remove it instead. In total 145 types and members are never used in the example solution – and they might hold on to references to assemblies that are not compatible for our migration. Careful with removing unused classes if you use dependency injection and assembly scanning for autowiring as you might get false positives with the Inspect tool.

Once those steps are completed and we have confirmed that the solution builds correctly and all tests are successful, we can then proceed to analyze the reference assemblies using a similar approach.

Removing Unused References

In order to avoid false positives during the assembly analysis, it is recommended to remove any unused references. This is just as easily done as mentioned earlier – unless you dynamically load assemblies. ReSharper might accidentally remove assemblies that are being used – so tests are going to be important to make sure that we don't remove significant references. If you know that you are loading assemblies dynamically, or you are unsure, be careful with removing assemblies. Make a copy, or better, as suggested earlier, use source control and make commits between changes.

Since we need fine-grained control, we are going to do this one project at a time, centered around the Main project and its dependencies. In the following examples, I'm going to use the BL.Main project.

Select a project and select main menu ➤ Extensions ➤ ReSharper ➤ Find ➤ Optimize References or use the shortcut Ctrl+Alt+Y.

The result will show different groups depending on the result. For example (Figure 3-9):

- Unused references

- Used references

- Implicit used references

- Unused packages with used dependencies

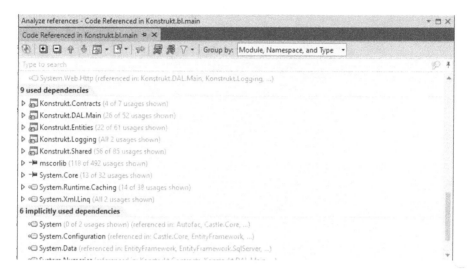

Figure 3-9. *Assemblies referenced in Konstrukt.BL.Main*

We are going to remove the unused references by selecting the ones we want to remove. If you select the Remove Unused References icon in the menu in the Analyze References window, you might end up with a few surprises. I highly recommend going through them one by one. When they are removed, ReSharper will also delete redundant namespace import directives in the project.

Let's take a look at another project. The Shared project. Our goal is to review the "Used References" tab and identify any assemblies that are not frequently used and can be removed without difficulty (Figure 3-10).

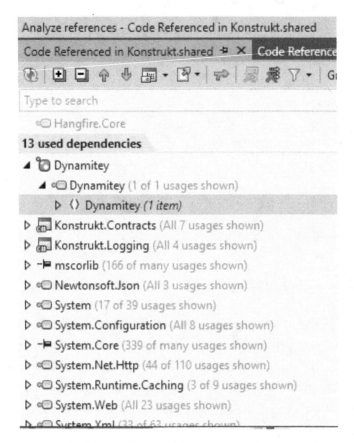

Figure 3-10. *Assemblies referenced in Konstrukt.Shared*

For this project there is a library Dynamitey (I will get back to this one later) that is used only once – might be worth looking at the usage and deciding if we need the library. I'll leave it for now. If you have an assembly that says "showing 0 of X usages," you can take a look at the code dependent on that assembly by using ReSharper. Locate the project in Solution Explorer, and under References find the reference in question and select Find Dependent Code (Figure 3-11).

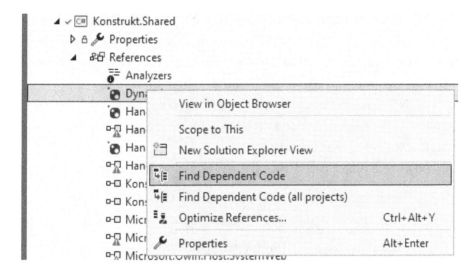

Figure 3-11. *Find dependent code option*

The information can help you figure out if the assembly is important, can be replaced, or be removed.

Repeat the preceding steps for all the projects, making sure to clean and build the solution, and run the tests again after each modification. Verify the solution builds and tests are green, and commit the changes. Take notes and organize them by project and/or namespace. We are going to need the notes later.

Analysis and Inventory

We have multiple tools available for the analysis phase of the migration. A former tool, Portability Analyzer has been deprecated, and many of the features have been included in the Upgrade Assistant which is the recommended replacement. At the time of writing, you can still use the Portability Analyzer tool, but the back-end service is not there anymore and therefore the tool has to be run while offline. The upgrade assistant has two main features, analysis, and upgrade. While the analysis is helpful in planning a migration, and we will take a look at it, there is another tool

37

that gives us an in-depth analysis, the .NET Update Planner. It wouldn't surprise me if this tool is combined with upgrade assistant at some point due to a lot of similarities that come up, but at the time of writing these are two separate tools and we will take a look at them both.

The .NET Planner can be found here `https://apisof.net/upgrade-planner`, as well as on GitHub as it is an open source project `https://github.com/dotnet/apisof.net`.

The overall difference between the two is the following:

> Upgrade planner: Generates comprehensive, high-level reports and actionable insights for planning.

> Upgrade assistant: Produces detailed, interactive reports with specific tasks and automated code fixes for immediate implementation.

Download the executable and run it, and select the folder or project depending on the size of your solution. The analysis itself might take some time as it scans the IL (Intermediate Language) of the binaries and looks it up against an API catalogue. The output is presented in a simple, yet easy to understand, three-window display (Figure 3-12).

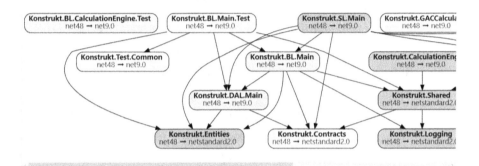

Figure 3-12. *Results for Konstrukt*

In the first window, we can see the list of assemblies and the portability score. The score isn't 100% accurate, so don't focus too much on that. The analyzer will even highlight issues with running on a different platform, such as Linux, which might not break until run although everything builds fine. In the problems window, we can see the following issues:

- API is not available on all platforms.

- AppDomain not available on .NET Core.

- System.Web not available on .NET Core.

- Unresolved references.

System.Web is expected and we will sort that out later. The real Konstrukt solution has more issues than the ones shown and also some back-end services that have old dependencies that could not be migrated which I have faked in the example we are using. I've used Konstrukt. ReportingService as an example as it relies on an old version of OpenXML as well as Windows specific assemblies and features such as System. Messaging and System.ServiceProcess. The service, however, relies on some of the shared libraries, such as Konstrukt.Logging, Konstrukt.Shared, Konstrukt.Contracts, and Konstrukt.Entitites. Although we could sort this out with refactoring, we are going to pretend that is not an option. Therefore, these will be migrated to .NET Standard as an intermediary step (we will cover alternatives). We can change the target framework by selecting the assemblies, right-clicking, and setting target to .NET Standard 2.0. The reason why we are not targeting .NET Standard 2.1 is that it does not support the .NET Framework. Specifically, .NET Standard 2.0 supports .NET Framework versions 4.6.1 and later, making it a more compatible choice for projects that need to maintain interoperability with existing .NET Framework code. This ensures broader compatibility while allowing for some of the newer features available in .NET Standard. If you already use net standard for projects, you should aim to retarget to the latest possible version. For libraries that need to support multiple older platforms, including .NET Core 3.x, Xamarin, and Mono, 2.1 would be a great option. .NET Standard, as mentioned earlier, is not deprecated. .NET Standard is still needed for some of our libraries due to reliance on .NET framework due to dependencies. Konstrukt.ReportingService which uses OpenXML and due to breaking cannot update (fictive example based on real-world scenario). However, .NET Standard is not recommended as "default." Use the latest version of .NET or at least .NET 6, if you can.

Select the assemblies that are your own; for other assemblies, we will look for replacements using a different tool. Since Konstrukt prefixes all the assemblies with Konstrukt, we can simply sort by name, select everything else, and remove by right-clicking.

To get a more accurate result, we will also set the desired framework and platform as following:

- Shared libraries: .NET Standard

- Reporting service: Leave as-is (.NET4.8)

- The rest: .NET 9

The result of the analysis can be saved as a project file, and you can even save the catalog offline. I'm going to export it as an excel file (Figure 3-13) and save it for later. I find the excel sheets easier to work with, so let's have a look. There are four tabs with the first one, assemblies, giving us an overview similar to the one we saw in the tool. The second tab, dependencies, lists the dependencies, and this tab is useful for looking up newer libraries that support the framework we want to target. The third tab, problems, is the most interesting tab as it lists all the specific problems that we have. You can filter the problems to exclude the ones we wanted to exclude earlier so we can get a clear overview over the work that needs to be done. The last tab lists the used APIs.

Assembly	Target Framework	Desired Framework	Desired Platforms	Score
Konstrukt.BL.CalculationEngine.Test	net48	net9.0	Any	100
Konstrukt.BL.Main	net48	net9.0	Any	100
Konstrukt.BL.Main.Test	net48	net9.0	Any	100
Konstrukt.CalculationEngine	net48	net9.0	Any	79.4
Konstrukt.Contracts	net48	netstandard2.0	Any	100
Konstrukt.DAL.Main	net48	net9.0	Any	100
Konstrukt.Entities	net48	netstandard2.0	Any	89.3
Konstrukt.GACCalculator	net48	net9.0	Any	100
Konstrukt.Logging	net48	netstandard2.0	Any	86.2
Konstrukt.ReportingService	net48	net48	Windows	100
Konstrukt.Shared	net48	netstandard2.0	Any	99.5
Konstrukt.SL.Main	net48	net9.0	Any	67.8
Konstrukt.SL.Notification.IntegrationTest	net48	net9.0	Any	100
Konstrukt.Tenancy	net48	net9.0	Any	100
Konstrukt.Test.Common	net48	net9.0	Any	100

Assemblies   Dependencies   Problems   Used APIs

Figure 3-13. *Generated report*

The percentage is an approximation that should be taken with a grain of salt. A score of 98% might be as much work as 70% depending on what the problems are. If a library is missing, and there is no good replacement, you might have to spend more time on those 2% than the rest.

Analyzing the Analysis

Once you have completed the initial analysis using your preferred target frameworks and platforms, review the problems and take note of their significance.

Based on the Konstrukt example, we see the following issues.

Unresolved References

Unresolved references to the following libraries:

- Nunit.framework

- Autofac (several)

- Log4net

- OpenXML

- Dynamitey

- Microsoft.VisualStudio.TestPlatform.TestFramework

System.Web Not Available on .NET Core

This one is a given and expected. I mentioned earlier that we could ignore System.Web; the detail tab explains this:

> *System.Web has been replaced by ASP.NET Core. You can fix many of the differences by adding a reference to System.Web. Adapters. If you are using .NET Upgrade Assistant to upgrade your project, this will be done automatically.*

To filter them out, we can utilize the filter dropdown for the column.

API Is Missing

Most of our issues here are related to System.Data.Entity and modeling the database objects.

The API Is Supported on Any Platform Except the Browser

We are using the ConfigurationManager and AppSettings, which are not available on any platform except the browser. This is commonly relevant for Blazor WebAssembly applications or other scenarios where .NET code runs directly in the browser via WebAssembly. Although Konstrukt doesn't have any current plans involving Blazor, we do want to have the option in the future.

The API Is Only Supported on These Platforms: Windows >= 6.1

The ReportingService generates graphs by using System.Drawing which is only supported on Windows 6.1 and up. If we want to target other platforms, we need to find an alternative.

The type and amount of issues will vary greatly from solution to solution, but what is important is that you go through the results and write some notes in regard to what needs work. If you use third-party dependencies that you'd like to migrate, you could use the tool to scan those as well. But we aren't done with the analysis quite yet. We are going to use a second tool.

Upgrade Assistant

We talked about the Upgrade Assistant and how it differs from the Upgrade Planner, and we're now going to use the assistant to generate similar reports as those are generated by the upgrade planner. You can find the Upgrade Assistant here: `https://github.com/dotnet/upgrade-assistant/tree/main`.

The tool supports the following project types:

- ASP.NET MVC

- Windows Forms

- Windows Presentation Foundation (WPF)

- Console app

- Libraries

- UWP to Windows App SDK (WinUI)

- Xamarin.Forms to .NET MAUI

Install the Upgrade assistant by running the following line in the terminal

```
dotnet tool install -g --add-source https://api.nuget.org/v3/
index.json --ignore-failed-sources upgrade-assistant
```

The --ignore-failed-sources flag is not always necessary but can be useful in certain situations. It tells the dotnet tool to continue with the installation even if some sources (like specific package feeds) fail to respond or are unreachable. This flag is particularly helpful when you're working in environments where you might have multiple NuGet sources configured, and some might be temporarily unavailable.

To analyze the solution:

```
upgrade-assistant analyze <path to solution file or project>
```

The analyzer will then ask you what you want to analyze, and we will select Application sources.

For the "What is your preferred target framework," we will choose .NET 8 which is the latest version at the time of writing. Follow the steps required by the tool.

```
What do you want to analyze in the selected projects?
> [X] Source code and settings
  [ ] Binary dependencies
```

After building and analyzing the projects, the tool will generate a file with the result, which might take some time. The result for Konstrukt can be seen in Figure 3-14. If you select HTML as the file output, you get an easy-to-navigate webpage with the result (Figure 3-15).

Figure 3-14. *Portability summary for Konstrukt*

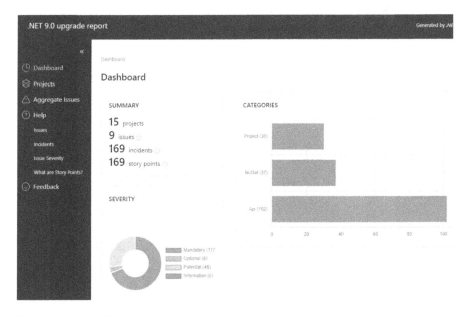

Figure 3-15. *Generated dashboard*

If we look at the aggregate issues, we can see similar issues to those found in the report generated by the Upgrade Planner. However, we see some we haven't seen before. Here are some.

API Available in NuGet Package

In older versions of .NET frameworks, certain APIs were transferred to separate NuGet packages that can now be included in projects as NuGet packages.

NuGet Package Is Incompatible

You'll find a list of packages that need to be upgraded or replaced. In our list, we see a few we didn't see earlier such as ApplicationInsights.

NuGet Package Upgrade Is Recommended for Selected Target Framework

For optimal compatibility, it is recommended to match the versions of .NET packages with the version targeted by your project. This isn't mandatory but recommended.

There are other issues, mostly focused on NuGet packages and retargeting, and of course upgrading the project file to the SDK style.

Let's take a closer look at the third-party dependencies we have to sort out.

Unresolved References

Autofac

Autofac is a dependency injection library, and after a quick search I can confirm that it works fine with the latest .NET. I used `https://www.nuget.org/` to look up the packages, but you can use Visual Studio Nuget

Window. There is also NuGetPackageExplorer which gives detailed information about NuGet packages. You can find the tool on GitHub: `https://github.com/NuGetPackageExplorer/NuGetPackageExplorer`.

Dynamitey

Dynamitey is an old open source library for working with dynamic objects. At the time of our migration, there weren't any .NET Core packages available, and although this has since changed, it underscored the fact that dependencies come with a cost. Our analysis revealed that Dynamitey was used only once in one project, which presented an opportunity to remove it by replacing the code with our own implementation. This would eliminate a dependency and reduce the potential workload in future migrations. To gauge the amount of work required to remove the Dynamitey dependency, let's revisit the code where it's used. Here's an example:

```csharp
public static class Extensions
{
    public static dynamic ToDynamicObject(this Dictionary
    <string, object> data)
    {
        dynamic dynamicData = new ExpandoObject();
        foreach (var kvp in data)
        {
            Dynamic.InvokeSet(dynamicData, kvp.Key,
            kvp.Value);
        }
        return dynamicData;
    }
}
```

We seem to mainly use the InvokeSet and InvokeGet on the Dynamic type. These two members dynamically invoke the set and get members using the Dynamic Language Runtime (DLR). And we can do that ourselves. We will need some tests as well, so a little bit of work is required.

EntityFramework

EntityFramework(EF), a popular ORM .NET mapper, is a completely different story – we use it heavily and even if we wanted to remove it, we wouldn't be able to do so without a significant rewrite. There is a .NET Core version of EF – but EF Core is a complete rewrite of EF, and there are many significant differences between the two. It should not be considered an upgrade. And if you have been using an EDMX model, like we have, then there is even more work. Besides the migration itself, you should expect a lot of time spent testing. The behavior is different, and you might not discover problems until you test all aspects.

To summarize, you have three options in regard to Entity Framework:

- Migrate to EF Core

- Use a different ORM (we have used Dapper in some of our new .NET Core services)

- Migrate to ASP.NET Core but target the full framework

As long as you target the full framework, you can also do a side by side, and run both versions: EF Core and EF6.

The team agreed on the following approach: some services will target the full .NET Framework until we can migrate to EF Core and replace EF with a slimmer option such as Dapper in services where we don't really use EF for more than object mapping. It's worth mentioning, however, that while Dapper is a lightweight and efficient micro-ORM, it lacks the extensive features provided by a full-fledged ORM like Entity Framework. This difference may impact the migration approach, especially for services that depend on more advanced ORM capabilities.

Log4Net

Later versions of Log4Net support .NET Standard 2.0, but we were worried about the lack of activity in the repository. Earlier issues with other types of logging than file logging had already made us cautious, so we decided to use NLog instead. Since we have abstracted away the logging, we shouldn't have to do too much work.

Microsoft.ApplicationInsights

Application Insights is a service that Azure provides for application monitoring. It consists of powerful analytics tools and a query language known as Kusto. We use it for performance monitoring, host diagnostics, error monitoring, and more.

Incompatible APIs

The original list was very long, but when we took a closer look, it wasn't as daunting. We have to update the project(s) we are migrating to the new SDK style project file, update dependencies, migrate shared libraries to .NET Standard, rewrite some code, and change how we access configuration items.

Some of the types used that require rewriting:

- MemoryCache

- HttpContext

- SQLClient (some unsupported members)

- ExceptionHandlerContext

- Any type from System.Drawing

After some investigation, we can conclude the following.

Caching is going to require some rewriting. For .NET Standard, there is Microsoft.Extensions.Caching.Memory, but the members are quite different and we will have to rewrite our cache management. It requires some work, but doable. ASP.NET Core MemoryCache is different from the MemoryCache object in the .NET assembly. There are fewer members available, and you cannot iterate over the cache items. We could explore other options, but at the moment Microsoft.Extensions.Caching.Memory seems like a good enough replacement.

The HttpContext isn't directly accessible anymore in ASP.NET Core. Instead, we will inject the context by using dependency injection. This doesn't require much work at all and is an easy fix that improves our code.

SQLClient has some members that are unsupported, but the Microsoft team has been actively working on this issue, and with some temporary workarounds, we should be able to make this work without too much trouble.

For global exception handling in ASP.NET Core, we will need to implement a middleware. Not much work, but it requires some testing.

The GAC

One issue that neither of the analyzers picked up was the reliance on an assembly in the GAC (Global Assembly Cache). The GAC is a special directory on the computer where shared .NET assemblies are stored. It allows multiple applications to share libraries, which can help reduce the overall footprint of the applications and ensure that they use the same version of a shared library. With .NET Core and later versions, the shift to NuGet packages and self-contained deployments has made the GAC obsolete. We will deploy the library with the projects that depend on it.

Summary

In this chapter, we did an in-depth analysis and collected data on the work required to do a migration. We have concluded that a migration is doable, although our ReportingService will continue to target 4.8. We know that we have some services that are going to be harder to migrate and that we will need to redo parts of our data access layer if we want to run ASP.NET Core on .NET Core. Now we have a clear understanding of the tasks ahead, and in the following chapter, we can start the process of planning our migration.

CHAPTER 4

Planning the Architecture

Before we start migrating, it's worth spending some time planning the migration based on what we learned from the analysis we did. Having a plan will save us time and pain. You certainly don't want to embark on a large migration, only to realize halfway through that the approach was wrong and that it's not going to work. In this chapter, we are going to cover options and considerations.

Migration Path

There are two recommended paths for migrating: full migration or incremental migration. Each approach has its own set of advantages, challenges, and best-use scenarios. Let's explore these paths in more detail, particularly in the context of Konstrukt's migration to embrace new features such as Minimal APIs and gRPC.

Full Migration

A full migration is done in one go, often by using the Upgrade Assistant, and can work well for smaller solutions with good compatibility. The migration itself is done in place, or by starting with a blank canvas (a new solution) and moving the old code over.

© Iris Classon 2024
I. Classon, *Migrating ASP.NET Microservices to ASP.NET Core 8*,
https://doi.org/10.1007/979-8-8688-1026-8_4

Advantages and Challenges

One-Time Effort

From a management perspective, this is a powerful selling point. Instead of maintaining two systems, you allocate more resources and effort toward migrating everything at once. However, this is also high risk as you'd have to delay other work as a full migration is resource intensive.

Consistency and Cleaner Architecture

Creating a cleaner solution is easier without the constraints of legacy code. In theory anyway, because this could easily backfire. Downtime can lead to pressure to produce, which in turn can impact decision-making resulting in rushed coding and shortcuts.

Incremental Migration

The incremental migration is done by using a temporary proxy service, YARP (Yet Another Proxy Service), while migrating the code little by little using the Stranger Fig Pattern. The Strangler Fig Pattern is a design pattern used for the gradual replacement of a legacy system with a new system. The term takes inspiration from the growth pattern of a strangler fig plant, which wraps around and ultimately replaces an established tree.

Incremental migration is less risky, but until the migration is complete, there will be more complexity and integration overhead.

Advantages and Challenges

Reduced Risk and Flexibility

The biggest advantage is reduced risk. By migrating bits and pieces, testing in-between and allowing enough time to discover issues, we reduce risk and can choose what, when, and how to migrate as we go. On the other hand, dealing with two systems adds integration overhead and complexity, and the migration process can take long and may face the risk of being given lower priority in the long term.

I will address both full and incremental migration in this book.

What to Migrate

Decide early on what platforms you want to target, particularly if you want to target cross-platform – or at least have the possibility to do so further down the line. Obviously, if you target cross-platform or a non-Windows platform, you won't be able to use ASP.NET Core targeting the full .NET platform. But you could mix if you have a distributed system that has different platforms available.

Migrating Everything

If you have a system that is smaller in size or complexity, or has few dependencies that are not supported, then this option could be for you. Your options are to either target .NET Core directly or target .NET Standard in your libraries and use ASP.NET Core for the web API services.

Mixed Systems

If you, like us, have a large system with intertwined services and/or complex system, then a mixed-mode system could be a better option, with or without a YARP proxy. Some services are left as is, shared dependencies target .NET standard, and what can be migrated to latest version of .NET is migrated one service at the time, by breaking out new services or all in one go.

If you are going to maintain a mixed system, you have to decide if you are going to maintain one shared library that targets .NET Standard, alternatively maintaining separate libraries. Sharing libraries is usually preferred if a lot of the code can be shared, and code that differs can be managed with conditional compilation and preprocessor symbols or by using the adapter design pattern. However, it's important to note that this approach can also introduce potential drawbacks. For instance, using conditional compilation and preprocessor symbols might reduce code readability, making it harder for developers to understand the code at a glance. Additionally, maintaining such code can become more complex, especially as the number of conditions grows or as the system evolves over time. These factors should be weighed against the benefits of shared code to determine the best approach for your project.

Strategic Considerations

When planning a migration, several strategic considerations should be taken into account to ensure a smooth transition. It is essential to have a comprehensive meeting with your team, product owners, and other stakeholders involved in the migration to identify specific considerations relevant to your scenario. In the following subsections, I will cover some key points to help guide your discussion.

Resources

Working at a startup, we had a small team that was constantly changing in size (scaling up and down depending on season and financial situation). We have to balance new features to keep our customers and investors happy, with maintenance and managing unintended features (bugs). If we do any sort of rewrite or migration, we have to manage that at the same time as we are doing everything else, and we cannot afford more than a couple of fulltime human resources on a migration or rewrite. Besides the number of available developer hours, you also have to think about knowledge resources. We talked about this earlier, and it's important to remember that development will slow down for a while until everybody catches up knowledge wise. You could aim for a few developers that have in-depth knowledge and can help and guide the other developers, or you could get everybody up to date. The choices made by you and your team are influenced by the team's size, division of work, and long-term goals.

Self-Contained Deployment or Framework Dependent

When you've decided whether to migrate everything or opt for a mixed system, you'll also need to make an important decision about the deployment strategy: whether to use Self-Contained Deployment (SCD) or Framework-Dependent Deployment (FDD). When you publish ASP.NET Core services, you can choose between framework-dependent deployment and self-contained deployment. As a quick refresher, self-contained means that your published package will have everything you need to run the service, while the framework-dependent publish will require you to prepare the environment beforehand and install the frameworks. Which one you choose depends on how you manage the environments the service gets deployed to, your user base, as well as whether you have size restrictions on your deployment packages. Konstrukt decided on Framework-Dependent Deployment (FDD) as we have a complex pipeline set up that manages our deployment really well.

When choosing between Self-Contained Deployment (SCD) and Framework-Dependent Deployment (FDD), consider your specific deployment scenario. SCD is ideal for environments you don't control, as it includes all dependencies, ensuring consistent operation across different systems. This is useful for applications deployed in varied or client-controlled environments.

FDD, on the other hand, is better suited for controlled environments where you can manage and ensure the correct .NET runtime is installed. It offers smaller deployment packages and centralized runtime management, making it efficient for enterprise applications with consistent deployment environments. The choice hinges on your control over the deployment environment, the need for consistency, and the importance of deployment size.

Here is a summary of the pros and cons.

Self-Contained Deployment (SCD)

Pros

- Environment needs less preparation and maintenance

- Ready-to-run packages

- Side-by-side installments

Cons

- Larger packages

- Publishing can take longer

Framework-Dependent Deployment (FDD) is still a popular and viable deployment model with the following pros and cons.

Framework-Dependent Deployment (FDD)

Pros

- Smaller deployment package. The .NET runtime is shared among applications and is not included in the deployment package.

- Centralized runtime management

Cons

- Deployment complexity. Ensuring the correct runtime version is installed on target machines can add complexity.

- Inconsistent Runtime Environment. Inconsistent runtime environments can cause difficult-to-diagnose issues.

Note   In previous versions of ASP.NET Core and Visual Studio, there were some bugs when creating self-contained packages. If you come across these issues, make sure you have all the Visual Studio updates and are running the latest .NET Core SDK (or runtimes if you don't need the full SDK).

Architecture and Conventions

Lastly, let's not forget the many smaller decisions you need to make regarding the opinionated framework, ASP.NET Core, such as dependency injection and the logging abstractions. Besides that, there are many other differences that you should keep in mind when planning. Here is an incomplete list of things that differ in ASP.NET Core:

- Simplified project file: The project file has been simplified and can be opened and edited in Visual Studio without first unloading the project.

- Bootstrap mechanism: The apps have a different bootstrap mechanism, and Global.asax doesn't exist anymore. Earlier versions used Startup.cs for configuration, but from ASP.NET Core 6.0 onward, a minimal hosting model centralizes setup in Program.cs.

- Main method and startup class: The startup class is loaded through the main method (similar to a console app) in the Program.cs file.

- Static files: Static files are stored in wwwroot, but can be configured to be stored in a different directory.

- Configuration management: Configuration data can be stored in different file formats, such as JSON files. Instead of the ConfigurationManager.AppSettings, you use the Configuration class that implements IConfiguration to get a section with GetSection. You can also provide a class to map configuration items by using the built-in dependency injection.

- Dependency injection: ASP.NET Core has built-in dependency injection, but you can provide your own container resolver (I'll show you how to use Autofac).

- Logging providers: ASP.NET Core has built-in logging providers, but you can provide your own.

- File providers: File access is done through File Providers, and these are used for everything from exposing the content root to locating pages and views (when using Razor Pages).

- Localization: App localization is simplified with IStringLocalizer, which uses the ResourceManager and ResourceReader to manage the culture.

- HttpContext access: HttpContext is accessed through IHttpContextAccessor instead of referencing HttpContext.Current directly (I will show you how to inject the context in third-party libraries that are dependent on the HttpContext object).

- OWIN and middleware: ASP.NET Core supports OWIN and utilizes middleware heavily, and it's easy to plug in your own middleware (at a slight performance cost).

- Middleware pipeline configuration: The order of middleware components can significantly impact the behavior of the application. Ensure proper configuration, especially for security-related middleware.

- Environment-specific settings: Use the IHostingEnvironment interface to manage environment-specific settings and configurations.

- Security best practices: Implement HTTPS enforcement, data protection, and proper authentication/authorization mechanisms to secure your application.

- Health checks: Utilize built-in health checks to monitor the application's health and dependencies.

- Versioning and compatibility: Plan for API versioning to handle changes and ensure backward compatibility.

Summary

In this chapter, we've taken a look at the migration options that we have and made some decisions in regard to the system we are migrating. We are going to do a partial migration, targeting .NET Core, and opt out of doing a self-contained deployment. There are also smaller decisions that we need to make concerning the architecture and conventions, but we will save that for the next chapter and cover them as we do the migration.

CHAPTER 5

Migration Part 1: In-Place Migration

I have experience with a wide range of migrations and rewrites, and it seems that most developers will eventually find themselves in a similar situation. The ever-changing landscape of technology is causing user expectations to grow at a fast pace. This is because there is now a vast selection of libraries and platforms to choose from. Not only is it tempting to migrate so we can try new solutions, but it is also often necessary to keep up with expectations and the growing technology stack. From my experience, migrations that ended poorly often shared the same issues: inadequate planning and a lack of clear goals. Fortunately for us, we have done an extensive analysis and planned the migration. By doing this, we can establish a roadmap that serves as a reference point for us to understand our current position and future destination. In this chapter, we will take a closer look at the migration paths we discussed in the previous chapter, as well as incorporate some of the new features in ASP.NET.

© Iris Classon 2024
I. Classon, *Migrating ASP.NET Microservices to ASP.NET Core 8*,
https://doi.org/10.1007/979-8-8688-1026-8_5

Yet Another Proxy (YARP)

YARP is a powerful and underrated library built by and for internal teams at Microsoft. It's an open source project developed by Microsoft that provides a highly customizable reverse proxy library for .NET applications. YARP is specifically designed to be a versatile and robust tool for developers who want to customize reverse proxy functionality. It is implemented on the top of the .NET Core infrastructure and supports ASP.NET Core 6.0 and up, and is provided as a NuGet package. YARP is a Layer-7 proxy (Figure 5-1) which means that it operates at the application layer of the OSI (Open Systems Interconnection) model, allowing it to inspect and manipulate the content of the traffic it handles. As an application layer proxy, it can terminate and reissue requests, do content-based routing (URL, host, header, cookie), do application aware load balancing, health checks, A/B testing, detailed logging and real-time monitoring and more. Other popular Layer-7 proxies are Nginx, HAPorxy, Envoy, and a few more. However, YARP stands out by being very customizable and highly flexible.

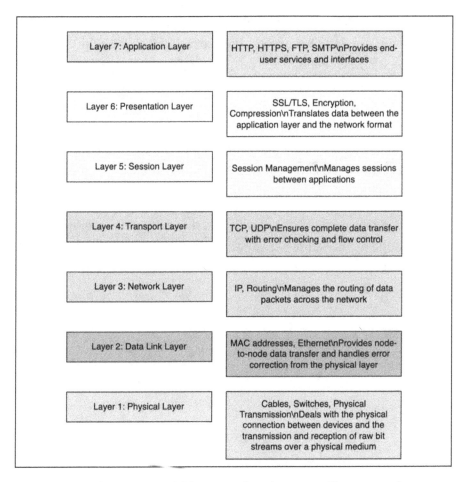

Figure 5-1. *The OSI model layers. This diagram illustrates the seven layers of the OSI model: physical, data link, network, transport, session, presentation, and application, detailing the functions of each layer in data communication*

There are a lot of use cases for a reverse proxy, and as a matter of fact, Konstrukt already uses a reverse proxy for load balancing and as a microservice gateway (routing requests to different microservices based on URL patterns) and API gateway (e.g., rate limiting based on client subscription model). In this book, we will use a combination of an incremental and full migration. We will use the upgrade assistant to migrate the libraries and use an incremental migration for the Web API applications. You don't have to use the proxy, but it's very helpful for complex systems, where in place migration is impossible, and for systems with intertwines UI, such as web forms. We will get back to the proxy in a little bit, but let's get started with migrating our libraries.

Migration Plan

This is the migration plan summarized from start to finish. The target framework has been highlighted with different colors in the .graphml graph as depicted in Figure 5-2. Once you have created a dependency graph in Visual Studio, you have the option to export the file and utilize it for planning purposes.

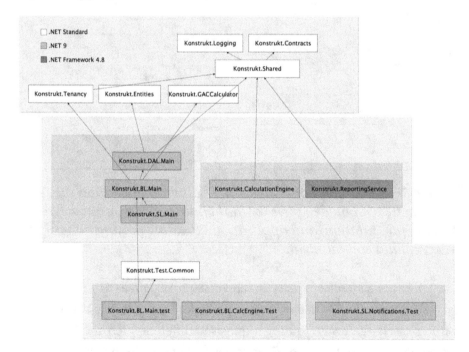

Figure 5-2. *Migration plan dependency graph. This graph shows the migration plan, with projects highlighted by target frameworks*

As mentioned earlier, we will start with the outer dependencies and work our way inward. These are our outer dependencies that should be fairly easy to migrate:

- Konstrukt.Contracts

- Konstrukt.Logging

Outer dependency with missing APIs:

- Konstrukt.GACCalculator

Working our way toward the web services, we have the tenancy and the shared library that has a consists of inner dependencies that require more work:

- Konstrukt.Tenancy

- Konstrukt.Shared

The following dependency requires significant work, possibly a complete rewrite:

- Konstrukt.Entities

The entities library will be a fair bit of work as we've identified that we need to migrate to a newer version of EF which doesn't support our edmx approach. We will migrate to code-first which means a different way of thinking.

Konstrukt.SL.Main web service stack as two layers, in addition to the ASP .NET Framework service:

- Konstrukt.DAL.Main

- Konstrukt.BL.Main

These cannot be migrated unless we have migrated the shared libraries and the Entities library. We'll get back to these later. Konstrukt.SL.Main will be migrated using YARP, and the CalculationEngine however, will be migrated to an ASP.NET Core gRPC service due to its need for high performance and efficient handling of large data streams.

Migrate using YARP:

- Konstrukt.SL.Main (Migrating to minimal APIs)

Migrate manually:

- Konstrukt.CalculationEngine (Migrating to gRPC)

Leave as is (targeting .NET 4.8)

- Konstrukt.ReportingService

Command Line Migration

The Microsoft Upgrade Assistant offers two methods for migration: using the command line or the Visual Studio extension, and we will explore both options. Currently, there is no notable distinction between the two options, so I suggest trying both and determining which one suits your migration needs best.

Using the command line, run the following:

```
upgrade-assistant upgrade -t Current .\{pathToYourSolution}.sln
```

Output

```
Which project do you want to upgrade?

> Konstrukt.BL.CalculationEngine.Test (Konstrukt.
BL.CalculationEngine.Test\Konstrukt.BL.CalculationEngine.
Test.csproj)
  Konstrukt.BL.Main (Konstrukt.BL.Main\Konstrukt.BL.Main.csproj)
  Konstrukt.BL.Main.Test (Konstrukt.BL.Main.Test\Konstrukt.
  BL.Main.Test.csproj)
  Konstrukt.CalculationEngine (Konstrukt.CalculationEngine\
  Konstrukt.CalculationEngine.csproj)
  Konstrukt.Contracts (Konstrukt.Contracts\Konstrukt.Contracts
  .csproj)
```

```
Konstrukt.DAL.Main (Konstrukt.DAL.Main\Konstrukt.DAL.Main
.csproj)
Konstrukt.Entities (Konstrukt.Entities\Konstrukt.Entities
.csproj)
...
```

We are going to select the Contracts library using the arrows on the keyboard and confirm with Enter. Konstrukt.Contracts is mostly interfaces and should be easy to migrate.

The next step prompts us to select the type of upgrade:

```
Steps
_____

Source project / Upgrade type
_____

How do you want to upgrade project Konstrukt.Contracts?

> Upgrade project to a newer .NET version
    In-place project upgrade (framework.inplace)
    Side-by-side project upgrade (framework.sidebyside)

  Upgrade project features
    Convert project to SDK style (feature.sdkstyle)
```

In-place upgrade modifies the existing project. The changes are immediate; there are no in-between steps and therefore generally faster. Side-by-side generates a new project, and therefore the risk is lower and roll-back is easier. Regardless of approach, always make a git commit right before you hit Enter, making sure you have a rollback point. During the analysis, we determined that in-place would be the best option for outer dependencies as they would be easy to migrate.

The next step is to select target framework:

Steps

Source project / Upgrade type / Target framework

What is your preferred target framework?
  .NET 6.0 (Supported until November, 2024)
  .NET 7.0 (Supported until May, 2024)
  .NET 8.0 (Supported until November, 2026)
  .NET 9.0 (Try latest preview features)
  .NETStandard 2.0
  .NETStandard 2.1

We are going to target .NET Standard 2.0 as this library is used by legacy services that are not a part of our migration plan.

Steps

Source project / Upgrade type / Target framework / Upgrade

We have gathered all required options and are ready to do the upgrade. Do you want to continue? [y/n] (y): y
Succeeded
Complete: 17 succeeded, 0 failed, 0 skipped.

To confirm everything went well during the migration, we will do the following:

- Clean and build the library.

- Run the tests.

- Run the services dependent on the library. This is done by running the Postman tests which runs a set of requests targeting our endpoints.

If you right-click on the project and select Find Dependent Code (available via ReSharper extension), you will see which libraries and services are dependent on this project. Make sure you test those, and if everything is clear, commit and push, preferably to a separate migration branch.

Migrating Using the Visual Studio Extension

While I typically favor command line tools, I must admit that the Upgrade Assistant Visual Studio extension is user-friendly and intuitive. It's as simple as right-clicking on a project and selecting Upgrade. If the option isn't there, download the extension manually at `https://marketplace.visualstudio.com/items?itemName=ms-dotnettools.upgradeassistant` and restart Visual Studio.

The steps for execution are identical to those in the command line, but the output is presented in a more understandable format. We'll select Konstrukt.Logging, Upgrade, and watch the result as the tool goes through the migration steps which are outputted in detail in the Output Window. The upgrade of the Konstrukt.Logging library was successful, although we have identified two libraries that are incompatible with the new target framework.

```
Package 'Microsoft.ApplicationInsights.Web' does not support
target framework(s) 'netstandard2.0' for project ...
Package 'Microsoft.AspNet.WebApi.Core' does not support target
framework(s) 'netstandard2.0' for project ...
```

Using NuGet we can search for the package and hopefully find a newer version that meets our requirements, and Microsoft.ApplicationInsights latest stable version does support .NET Standard 2.0. As I'm sure you know, you can often get a little bit of extra help by right-clicking on a missing type inside the Visual Studio and get a suggestion for a package. However, this might not always work when you're migrating. For example, for the interface for the exception handler if I right-click and install the recommended NuGet package, I will get a warning that it doesn't support the target framework. If you accidentally install an unsupported package, simply uninstall it.

The second package was not as straightforward to replace and posed the first major challenge. Dealing with the exception handler, which is a common issue when migrating from ASP.NET to ASP.NET Core. In traditional ASP.NET, we used a global exception handler, which allowed us to centrally manage exceptions across the application. However, ASP.NET Core has shifted to using middleware for exception handling. This change requires a different approach, where exceptions are caught and handled within the middleware pipeline, providing more flexibility and control over how exceptions are managed and logged.

We have three options:

- Comment out the code until we migrate the service using it.

- Use conditional compilation.

- Abstract away the platform specific implementation.

- Move the code temporarily to the platform specific project.

Comment Out the Code Until Migration

This is a quick and straightforward method to proceed with other parts of the migration without being blocked by this issue. However, it comes with the drawback that exception handling will not be available, which can hinder debugging and error tracking during the transition phase.

Use Conditional Compilation

Conditional compilation is when we use preprocessor symbols, defined in our project file, that define scopes of code that are only compiled for the targeted platform. One of the main goals of .NET Standard is to provide a consistent API surface across different platforms. Extensive use of conditional compilation can undermine this goal, leading to code that behaves differently on different platforms.

Abstract Away the Platform-Specific Implementation

In my opinion, this is the most robust. By defining an interface in the .NET Standard library and providing platform specific implementation by dependency, we can maintain a clean and maintainable library that targets .NET Standard only.

Move the Code Temporarily to a Platform-Specific Project

Another approach is to temporarily move the platform-specific code to a project that targets the specific platform (e.g., a .NET Framework or .NET Core project). This allows you to maintain the shared library as a clean, cross-platform codebase without any conditional compilation. This option works well for code that can be easily broken out and can also be used with dependency injection as mentioned earlier. The exception handling is only used in SL.Main, and therefore we can simply move the exception handling classes to the SL.Main service (knowing that we will write this once we migrate the service). The real-world Konstrukt system uses this exception handling in several services, and we ended up creating a separate library for platform specific logging that implemented shared interfaces.

With all our issues solved, we rebuild, run the tests, and the requests, verifying everything is okay before we commit our latest changes to the Migration branch.

Migrating GAC Projects

The next project we want to migrate is the Konstrukt.GACCalculator, which is a made-up project to demonstrate a couple of migration issues you might run into. .NET 5 and later versions do not use the GAC. Instead, there's an emphasis on a modular approach, where each application is self-contained with its own dependencies. This design improves application isolation and reduces dependency conflicts (also known as "DLL Hell"). "DLL Hell" occurs when different applications update shared DLLs to incompatible versions, causing conflicts. This also greatly simplifies deployment, especially in containerized environments. Konstrukt.BL.Main uses the GAC assembly, and we can solve this by either

- Direct (project or assembly) reference

- NuGet reference

If the project is in the same solution, then we might as well use a direct project reference. If the assembly is in the GAC, it is likely an existing assembly that we don't have the code for, or it is in a separate solution or repository, in which case a NuGet package might be suitable. We are going to remove the GAC reference, and reference the project directly instead, before we proceed with the migration. Keep in mind that if a project is accessed through the GAC, then it won't show references in the project when you try to find dependent code. A file search for the assembly's name would however help you locate references.

After migrating the project, we find that some types are missing, for example, Bitmap. Migrating code that relies on System.Drawing (such as creating and manipulating images) to .NET Standard requires a different approach since System.Drawing is not fully supported in .NET Standard. You can use the System.Drawing.Common package, which provides cross-platform support for drawing in .NET Core and .NET 5+. I could even use the SkiaSharp library, or other graphics libraries.

Migrating Libraries with DbContext References

The Tenancy library, Konstrukt.Tenancy, has several references to EF types such as DbContext. Although this type exists in EF Core, we want to abstract away the dependency so the library can continue being shared by both new and old services. This is easily solved with an IDataStoreContext interface which allows the calling project to wire up their own target platform-specific database context.

In the shared Tenancy project:

```
public interface IDataStoreContext
{
    string ChangeInitialCatalog(string catalog);
    string ChangeConnectionString(string catalog);
}

public class MultiTenancyHandler : IMultiTenancyHandler
{
    readonly ICurrentRequest _currentRequest;

    public MultiTenancyHandler(ICurrentRequest currentRequest)
    {
        _currentRequest = currentRequest;
    }
}
```

In SL.Main:

```
public class DataStoreContext : IDataStoreContext
{
    private readonly DbContext _context;

    /// <summary>
    /// Initializes a new instance of the <see cref=
        "DataStoreContext"/> class.
    /// </summary>
    /// <param name="context">The DbContext instance that
        provides access to the database.</param>
    public DataStoreContext(DbContext context)
    {
        _context = context;
    }

    /// <summary>
    /// Changes the initial catalog (database name) in the
        current connection string
    /// and returns the updated connection string.
    /// </summary>
    /// <param name="catalog">The name of the new database to
        switch to.</param>
    /// <returns>The updated connection string with the new
        database name.</returns>
    public string ChangeInitialCatalog(string catalog)
    {
        // Logic for changing the catalog (database name) in
            the connection string
        return _context.Database.Connection.ConnectionString;
    }
```

```
/// <summary>
/// Updates the connection string with a new value.
/// </summary>
/// <param name="connectionString">The new connection
    string to use.</param>
/// <returns>The updated connection string, but currently
    returns an empty string.
/// This might need implementation or modification
    depending on the specific requirements.</returns>
public string ChangeConnectionString(string
connectionString)
{
    // Logic for changing the connection string omitted
    return connectionString;
}
}
```

SL.Main IoC Module (simplified code):

```
builder.Register(c =>
{
    var context = new KonstruktEntities2();
    context.Database.CommandTimeout = Shared.Constants.
    ServerTimeoutSeconds;
    c.Resolve<IMultiTenancyHandler>().UseTenantContext
    (new DataStoreContext(context));
    return context;
}).AsSelf().InstancePerDependency();
```

Migrating Entity Framework-Dependent Libraries

Next in line on our migration journey is the Konstrukt.Entities project where our entities have been created using a database-first approach and the EDMX designer (Figure 5-3). Our database objects are accessed through repositories with some shared methods and some custom methods. The use of repositories and a couple of layers of abstractions makes the migration easier.

Either we migrate to .NET Core and have all the services use Entity Framework Core, or we can run both side by side in the same project – but that can quickly get very messy, so we don't want to do that. We do however have to maintain two separate, but model-identical Entities libraries until we're done with migrating the rest of the solution. This ensures compatibility between the new .NET Core services and the legacy .NET Framework during migration and allows for gradual updates without disrupting existing functionality. The long-term plan is to consolidate these libraries into a single codebase once all services are migrated. If this approach is not feasible for you, an alternative approach would be to implement a layer of abstraction, like accessing the entities through a service.

Figure 5-3. Konstrukt.Entities was created using the EDMX approach, which generates classes that match the database schema, with or without customization

EF Core does not support the EDMX model, and there is no plan for supporting this in the future as code-first has become the de facto method. There are, however, tools you can use to get the visual aspects of working with the database.

These are three common approaches for working with a relational database such as Microsoft SQL Server:

- EDMX first: Uses a visual designer to create a model and generate database schema and classes.

- Database first: Uses an existing database schema to generate the model and classes.

- Code first: Defines the model in code and generates the database schema from the code.

We have three options moving forward:

- Generate a database from code using migrations (code first).

- Generate entities from the database using reverse-engineering.

- Hybrid approach where we use model configuration to keep the database and codebase in sync. Nothing is generated/scaffolded, and it is important to take extra precautions to ensure that the two are in sync.

While the idea of using a hybrid approach can be appealing, it does come with added complexity and multiple areas where things can go wrong. It remains an option for those who, for whatever reason, cannot use the former two methods. Per Microsoft's documentation, here is some advice for a hybrid approach.

Familiarize Yourself

Read guides on treating code and database as sources of truth to understand key considerations.

Skip Modeling Migrations

Since migrations aren't used, don't model sequences, non-primary indexes, constraints, or index filters.

Integration Testing

Use a robust test suite to ensure proper synchronization between code and database as they evolve.

Validate Mappings

Generate a dummy database with a throwaway migration and compare it to the actual database to identify schema differences.

Customize with Partial Classes: Optionally, generate partial classes from the database and use extensions for custom code configuration.

Scaffolding the Model

As we already have our database, we will be using the second option, scaffolding the model based on our database. I highly recommend you do this with a throwaway database first and create backups of the database. Rather safe than sorry, right?

Our first step is to migrate (right-click project ➤ Upgrade) the project to a side-by-side project, Konstrukt.Entities.Core, targeting the latest version of .NET. There are a few ways we can scaffold the model, and one of the options is in the form of a handy NuGet package. Using the Package Manager Console (Main menu ➤ Tools ➤ NuGet package Manager ➤ NuGet Package Manager Console) install the following:

`Microsoft.EntityFrameworkCore.Tools`

Set the new entities project as startup project, and use the following to scaffold:

`Scaffold-DbContext "Server=myServerAddress;Database=myDat aBase;User Id=myUsername;Password=myPassword;" Microsoft. EntityFrameworkCore.SqlServer`

`Microsoft.EntityFrameworkCore.SqlServer`

You might run into problems with missing SQL server assemblies, and if you do, use NuGet to find and add those packages. An alternative is EF Power Tools (Figure 5-4), a robust extension that simplifies many of the tasks associated with Entity Framework Core, such as reverse engineering, migrations, and model visualization. The tool can be downloaded from Visual Studio Marketplace:

`https://marketplace.visualstudio.com/items?itemName=ErikEJ. EFCorePowerTools` .

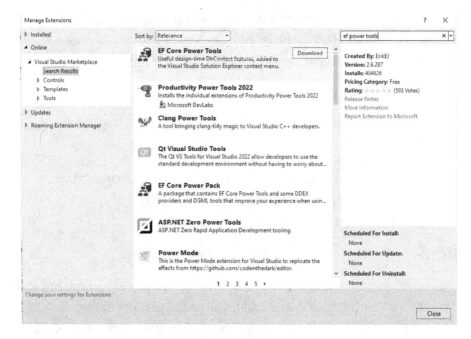

Figure 5-4. *EF Core Power Tools provides useful design-time DbContext features, scaffolding, and more*

After installing and restarting Visual Studio, right-click project and select EF Core Power Tools ➤ Reverse Engineer as shown in Figure 5-5.

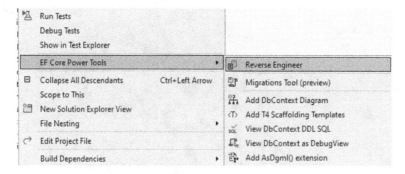

Figure 5-5. *The extension adds a menu option for the tool, with options such as Reverse Engineer*

Select or add data connection and EF Core version (Figure 5-6).

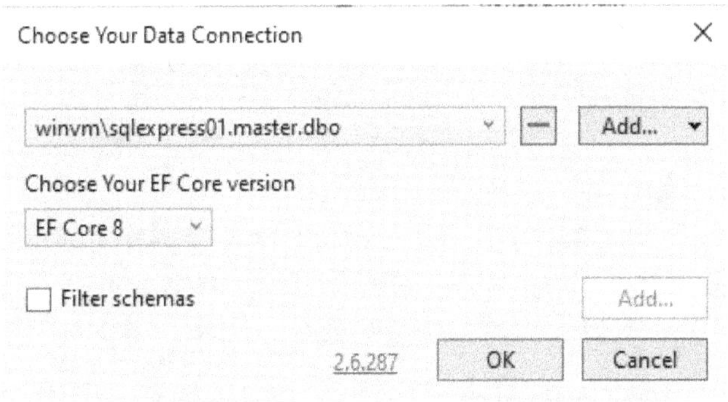

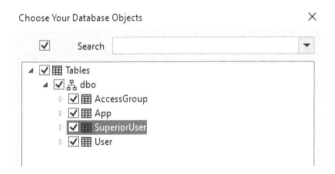

Figure 5-6. *This dialog box in EF Core Power Tools allows users to select a data connection and specify the EF Core version*

Select the database objects you want to reverse engineer (Figure 5-7).

Figure 5-7. *The next dialog box allows users to choose specific database objects*

Finally, we can choose our settings. We want to generate EntityTypes and DbContext (Figure 5-8).

Choose Your Settings for Project Konstrukt.Entities.Core   ✕

Context name | KonstruktEntities2 |

Namespace | Konstrukt.Entities.Core |

EntityTypes path (f.ex. Models) - optional
| Models |

What to generate | EntityTypes & DbContext   ⌄ |

Naming

☑ Pluralize or singularize generated object names (English)

☐ Use table and column names directly from the database

☐ Use DataAnnotation attributes to configure the model

☐ Customize code using templates | C# - T4   ⌄ |

☐ Include connection string in generated code

☐ Install the EF Core provider package in the project

Help ⋆ Rate

| Advanced... | | OK | | Cancel |

Figure 5-8. *This dialog box sets context name, namespace, and other generation options for EF Core models*

In the example configuration for the Konstrukt.Entities.Core project, the tool will generate a DbContext class named KonstruktEntities2, and the generated classes will be placed under the Konstrukt.Entities. Core namespace. Entity types will be organized into a folder named Models. Both EntityTypes and DbContext will be generated, and the tool will pluralize or singularize generated object names based on English conventions. The final result is very similar to what we had in Konstrukt. Entities, albeit without the EMDX model and diagram.

Adding a Layer of Abstraction

The next step is to make sure everything works as expected and that we are able to connect to the database and access the entities. There are a couple of ways to test this, but a simple console app targeting the latest version of .NET will do for a first test. Since we are going to maintain two entities projects side by side, we want to have a layer of abstraction when accessing the entities so that the two implementations implement the same interface.

In our IoC container, we can then simply swap out the implementation depending on the platform we are targeting. Therefore, The IRepository and IAppRepository are moved to the Konstrukt.Contracts library. The console app gets its own AppRepository implementation, as well as the abstract base class Repository<T> that implements the shared IRepository interface.

Subsequently, the repository classes can be registered in the ServiceCollection for the console app. The connection string, which I added as an environment variable, can also be retrieved there. As mentioned earlier, configuration data such as connection strings can be read from different sources such as console arguments, environment variables, and JSON or XML file. I'll cover the different configuration providers later on in the book.

The simple console app has a single purpose, and that is to let us test the connection and the repository layers in an isolated manner. Ideally, we would have integration tests for the target platforms. This can be done in one project by using conditional compilation; however, incorporating conditional compilation sporadically would lead to a cluttered codebase and is known for causing issues when compiling for different targets. For example, at the time of writing, conditional compilation was causing issues with Intellisense, global usings, and missing namespaces that were referenced.

All in all, conditional compilation for tests is not something I'd recommend. However, I have included a project in the source code, called DualPlatformEntitiesTest (Figure 5-9), as an example of what a project like that could look like.

```
DualPlatformEntitiesTest (net48)                                        ▼
 1  using Konstrukt.Contracts.Cache;
 2  using Konstrukt.Contracts.Repository;
 3  using Microsoft.Extensions.DependencyInjection;
 4  #if NET48
 5  using Konstrukt.Entities;
 6  using Konstrukt.DAL.Main.Repository;
 7  using Konstrukt.BL.Main.Util;
 8  #else
 9  using EntitiesConsoleTmp;
10  using Konstrukt.Entities.Core.Models;
11  #endif
12  using NUnit.Framework;
```

Figure 5-9. *Conditional compilation can be used anywhere in a class file, including namespaces*

Example test code:
using Konstrukt.Contracts.Cache;
using Konstrukt.Contracts.Repository;
using Microsoft.Extensions.DependencyInjection;
using NUnit.Framework;
#if NET48
using Konstrukt.Entities;
using Konstrukt.DAL.Main.Repository;
using Konstrukt.BL.Main.Util;
#else
using EntitiesConsoleTmp;
using Konstrukt.Entities.Core.Models;
#endif

```
namespace DualPlatformEntitiesTest {
    public class Tests {
        private ServiceProvider _serviceProvider;

        [SetUp]
        public void Setup() {
            var serviceCollection = new ServiceCollection();

#if NET48
            serviceCollection.AddScoped<IAppRepository<App>,
            AppRepository>();
            serviceCollection.AddScoped<KonstruktEntities2>
            (serviceProvider => new KonstruktEntities2());
            serviceCollection.AddScoped<ICacheHandler>(service
            Provider => new CacheHandler("local"));
            _serviceProvider = serviceCollection.BuildService
                                 Provider();
#else
            _serviceProvider = Program.CreateServices();
#endif
        }

        [Test]
        public void VerifyAppId()
        {
            var repository = _serviceProvider.GetService<IApp
                             Repository<App>>();
            var app = repository.GetByAppId("07054ace-86f5-4f7
                      a-9e14-8bed3c552cd0");
            Assert.AreEqual("Prognos", app.AppName);
        }
```

```
    [TearDown]
    public void TearDown() {
        _serviceProvider?.Dispose();
    }
  }
}
```

The tests can be run by using the command line:

```
dotnet test -f net48
dotnet test -f net8.0
```

Or by using a test runner that supports running tests for different target frameworks (Figure 5-10).

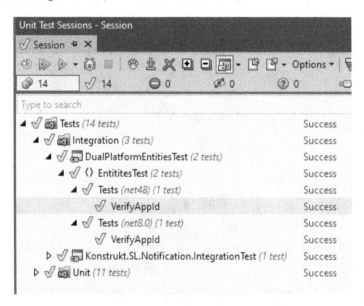

Figure 5-10. *Some test runners, such as Visual Studio test runner and ReSharper test runner, support running tests for multiple target platforms*

Summary

In this chapter, we've explored the initial phase of our migration journey, focusing on the in-place migration of various components. We discussed planning and goal setting, and I've introduced YARP, a highly customizable reverse proxy library by Microsoft, and its role in our migration strategy. We started the migration journey based on our detailed plan, starting with the outer dependencies such as Konstrukt.Contracts and Konstrukt. Logging, and moving toward more complex components like Konstrukt. Entities. Konstrukt.Entities required significant work due to its dependency on an older version of Entity Framework, but we had some help by tools such EF Core Power Tools for reverse engineering the database schema.

In the next chapter, we will continue the migration, focusing on the incremental migration of an ASP.NET service by using a reverse proxy.

CHAPTER 6

Migration Part 2: Incremental Migration

Incremental Migration Using YARP

Now that we have migrated the majority of the shared dependencies, we can start migrating the ASP.NET project and its direct dependencies: the business layer and the data access layer. An incremental migration can take a while, depending on the complexity of your project. Since we are using a reverse proxy to make calls to the legacy service, we don't have to rush the migration and can do it one controller at a time, or even more modularly if needed.

Creating the YARP Project

Our incremental migration starts with the ASP.NET project, and its upgrade options look a little different compared to the libraries we migrated earlier. After selecting Upgrade as we did previously and choosing "Update project to a newer .NET version," we only get the option to do an incremental upgrade as shown in Figure 6-1. Likewise, in the next step, there is only one option for the upgrade target, a new project (Figure 6-2).

© Iris Classon 2024
I. Classon, *Migrating ASP.NET Microservices to ASP.NET Core 8*,
https://doi.org/10.1007/979-8-8688-1026-8_6

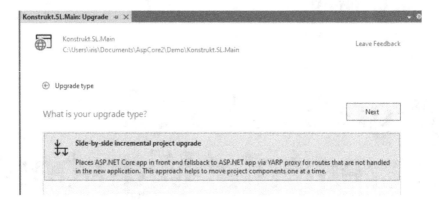

Figure 6-1. *This option allows the ASP.NET Core app to run alongside the legacy ASP.NET app, using YARP for unhandled routes*

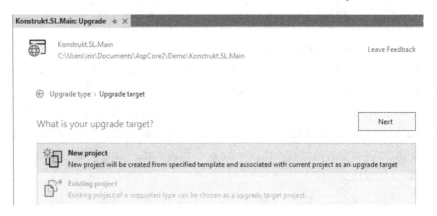

Figure 6-2. *Incremental upgrades for our ASP.NET service only allows "New project" as the upgrade target*

We'll name the project Konstrukt.SL.Main.Core and select ASP.NET Core Web API as project template (Figure 6-3). The Upgrade Assistant then runs through various internal steps, updating the status of the internal steps (Figure 6-4). The summary shows us how many endpoints were migrated and percentage currently running on .NET Framework vs .NET (Figure 6-5).

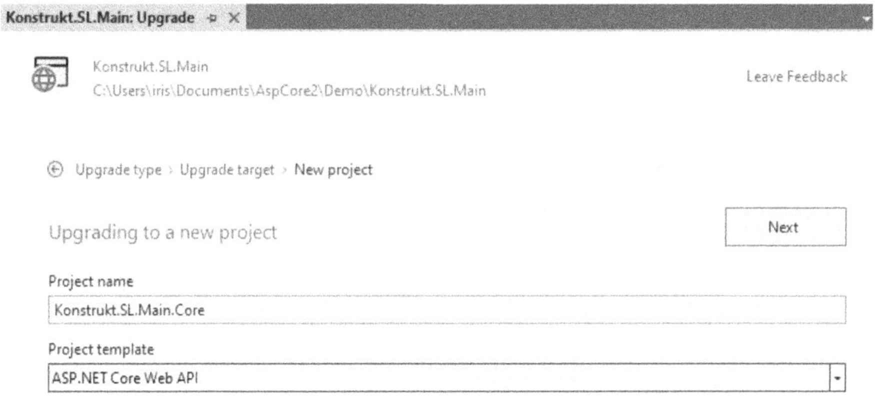

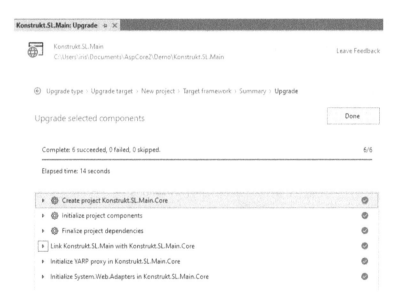

Figure 6-3. *In the final upgrade configuration step, we can add the name of the new project and the project template*

Figure 6-4. *Upgrade progress is shown as the tool runs through the internal steps. For a detailed output, check the Output Window in Visual Studio*

Figure 6-5. *The summary tab shows a summary of the migration*

The window for the Upgrade Assistant has several tabs such as the Endpoint Explorer (Figure 6-6). Endpoint Explorer shows all the endpoints, and we'll get back to this later during the migration. Endpoint Explorer is a powerful feature integrated in Visual Studio that we can use to explore endpoints, as well as create and save requests.

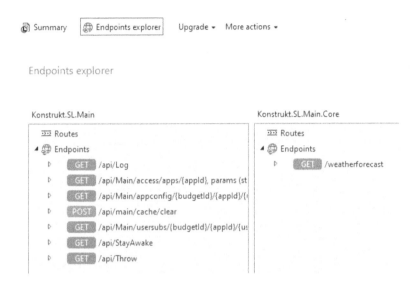

Figure 6-6. Endpoint Explorer is a powerful Visual Studio feature that lets us discover endpoints, create requests, and save them for later

Under the More actions tab, you can remove the upgrade, and with the Upgrade tab, we can migrate parts of the old project.

We now have an empty Web API project with a YARP proxy and a WeatherForecastController. My recommendation is to keep the controller there until you begin migrating the controllers from the legacy project, as a means of differentiating between the two for troubleshooting purposes. We will first run the project (with its built-in proxy service) and ensure that everything is functioning smoothly before we proceed with migrating our first controller.

You might run into the following error when you run the project the first time. By default, Visual Studio should set both the ASP.NET Core project and the legacy ASP.NET project as startup projects when the Upgrade Assistant finishes, but sometimes things happen.

```
Yarp.ReverseProxy.Forwarder.HttpForwarder: Information:
Request: An error was encountered before receiving a response.
```

95

```
System.Net.Http.HttpRequestException: No connection could
be made because the target machine actively refused it.
(localhost:{port})
```

Chances are that you don't have multiple startup projects configured. Right-click on the solution in Solution Explorer and select Configure Startup Projects. Select multiple and set the YARP project and the legacy project as startup projects (Figure 6-7).

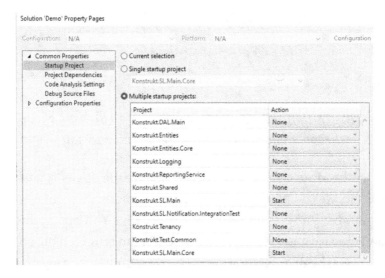

Figure 6-7. *For the YARP proxy to work the legacy, ASP.NET project must be running as well. Make sure both projects are set as startup projects*

With the services running, we can see the magic. My ASP.NET Core app is running on port 7056 and the legacy service on 52637. If I call the WeatherForecastController, I get the result from the controller in the ASP. NET Core YARP project, which is the only controller in our new project. And our legacy controllers work as expected when we run the collection of requests using Postman. However, if we call the same endpoints but use the ASP.Core port, we will get the same results even though the controllers have not been migrated yet. This is how it works: When a request doesn't find a matching endpoint in the ASP.NET Core project, YARP intercepts it and forwards it to the legacy ASP.NET application. The legacy app processes the request and sends the response back through YARP, which then relays it to the original client. Now that is the beauty of using a reverse proxy!

Note   Use HTTPS for the endpoints, double check the configuration in Startup.cs and that the MapForwarder has the correct pattern ("/{**catch-all}" works for most scenarios). In addition, verify profiles in launchSettings.json, in particular the ProxyTo.

To migrate the first controller, we will right-click it and select Upgrade (Figure 6-8). My suggestion is to start by migrating the simplest API controller that you have. The initial controller that needs to be migrated will always demand more effort, as we have to resolve the dependencies too.

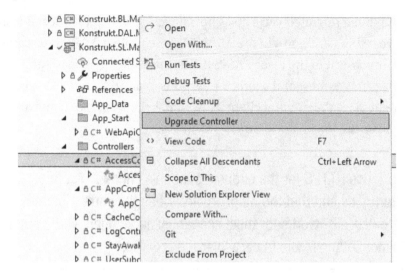

Figure 6-8. *Upgrading controllers can be done through the Upgrade tab in the Upgrade Assistant Window or the context menu for the project*

The next view will show us what we can migrate and allow us to select the controller including its dependencies, or pick specific components. We'll migrate the controller and everything that comes with it, knowing that we'll have to do some manual work to make the code compile.

Konstrukt.BL.Main target framework is incompatible (Figure 6-9). We can migrate the library in place, like we have done for the other libraries, but if we target .NET 8, it will force us to migrate the rest of Konstrukt. SL.Main in one go. We have two alternatives, migrate to .NET Standard 2.0 or migrate to a new project targeting .NET 8. From our analysis earlier, we know that this library has dependencies that won't work with .NET Standard, mainly EntityFramework Core. Therefore, we will migrate the library to a new project using the same steps as we've used earlier.

Figure 6-9. *Some of our dependencies cannot be automatically sorted out. For example, BL.Main still targets .NET 4.8*

The Upgrade Assistant does offer an option to do an incremental upgrade like the one we are doing with the proxy app. A new project is created, Konstrukt.BL.Main.Core, a link is added to the original project, and we can migrate one or several classes at the time. I'm going to be completely honest here; this might just add more work and complexity to the mix.

When choosing a migration strategy, consider these factors:

- Application size and complexity: For large or complex applications, incremental migration is safer, allowing you to migrate in smaller, manageable steps.

- Resource availability: If you have the resources for parallel development, a side-by-side migration is quicker and more efficient.

Side-by-side migration is ideal for complex applications where maintaining the original project during the upgrade is crucial. Side-by-side incremental migration is particularly useful for web applications moving from ASP.NET to ASP.NET Core, enabling gradual migration while keeping the legacy system operational.

Generally, I recommend side-by-side migration for a cleaner, faster transition. However, if your application is large or you have limited resources, incremental migration might be the better option. With good source control and frequent commits, you can adjust as needed.

If we had started with one of the two libraries instead of the ASP.NET service, then we could have gone down the incremental path. Attempting to incrementally upgrade three projects concurrently can result in a lack of clarity and potential confusion. As you can see in Figure 6-10, only 3 out of 15 components could be migrated.

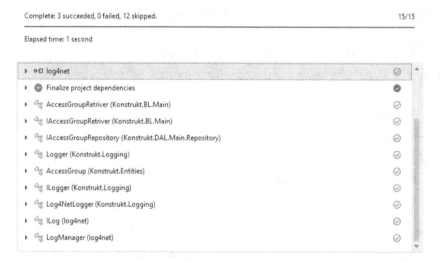

Figure 6-10. *When attempting to do an incremental upgrade of BL. Main, the summary tells us that only 3 out of 15 components could be migrated*

The project has after all a dependency on Konstrukt.DAL.Main, which is also targeting .NET 4.8. Do we do an incremental upgrade for that library as well? For Konstrukt it was easier to skip the incremental upgrade for the libraries, and instead migrate the withstanding libraries to copy-projects making sure to update project references to appropriate migrated projects, and NuGet packages to packages that support the new target framework.

Migrating an ASP.NET Service to ASP.NET Core

Before we continue with the incremental migration, let's do a short walkthrough of the ASP.NET Core project structure. While I assume some prior knowledge, a brief introduction is always helpful to refresh our memories. For more in-depth information, Microsoft documentation is a fantastic starting point and of course Apress books.

Project Structure

Here's a breakdown of the key components and file in a new ASP.NET Core project.

Dependencies

The References node in Solution Explorer shows all the NuGet packages and project references your project depends on. For an ASP.NET Core project, this typically includes frameworks such as Microsoft.AspNetCore. App and Microsoft.NetCore.App. Under NuGet packages, you'll find, unless you opted out, a Swashbyckle.AspNetCore package (we'll talk about this later in this chapter).

The Frameworks tab shows assemblies that are part of the .NET SDK. Since ASP.NET Core packages are included by the SDK, they appear under Frameworks rather than Packages. Similarly, if you examine the project file, you will notice that it only contains Swashbuckle references as a package, and the project SDK is Microsoft.NET.Sdk.Web. Under Analyzers, you'll see a wide range of analyzers.

```
<Project Sdk="Microsoft.NET.Sdk.Web">
  <PropertyGroup>
    <TargetFramework>net8.0</TargetFramework>
    <Nullable>enable</Nullable>
    <ImplicitUsings>enable</ImplicitUsings>
  </PropertyGroup>
  <ItemGroup>
    <PackageReference Include="Swashbuckle.AspNetCore"
    Version="6.4.0" />
  </ItemGroup>
</Project>
```

Properties Folder

Properties holds the launchSettings.json. This file contains settings that control how the application is launched. It includes profiles for different environments (e.g., IIS Express, Project) and environment variables.

Controllers Folder

As you know, controllers are the entry points for handling HTTP requests in your Web API, and the starter project always includes an example controller, which is currently the WeatherForecastController.cs.

App Settings

Configuration isn't done with a web or app config. File (although you can in theory still use an XML-based config file), rather it is done in a JSON file for improved readability. You'll see two nested files:

- appsettings.json: This file contains configuration settings for your application. It typically includes settings logging and third-party services. You can add connection strings in the JSON file, but it's not recommended to put any sensitive information in the settings file as you won't want that checked into you remote repository.

- appsettings.Development.json: This file contains environment-specific settings that override the settings in appsettings.json when the application is running in the Development environment. We'll cover working with settings later.

Program.cs

This is the main entry point for your application. It sets up the WebHost, configures services, and defines the middleware pipeline. It's the equivalent of Global.asax.cs and WebApiConfig.cs files in your legacy ASP. NET app. Starting with .NET 6, the Program.cs file handles both service configuration and middleware setup, which was traditionally done in the Startup.cs file. Here's an explanation of each part of the Program.cs code based on the default template setup:

```
var builder = WebApplication.CreateBuilder(args);
```

This line initializes a new instance of the WebApplicationBuilder, which provides the necessary services for the application and sets up configuration, logging, and dependency injection

```
builder.Services.AddControllers();
builder.Services.AddEndpointsApiExplorer();
builder.Services.AddSwaggerGen();
```

AddControllers() adds the necessary services for the MVC pattern (Model–View–Controller) which is used for creating API controllers in the application. AddEndpointsApiExplorer() adds support for discovering endpoints and generating OpenAPI (Swagger) documentation.

The AddSwaggerGen() method adds and configures the services required to generate Swagger documentation for the API.

```
var app = builder.Build();
```

This line builds the WebApplication instance from the builder, which will then be used to configure and run the application.

```
if (app.Environment.IsDevelopment()) {
app.UseSwagger();
app.UseSwaggerUI();
}
```

This code block configures middleware for the HTTP request pipeline. It checks if the environment is developed using app.Environment. IsDevelopment().

app.UseSwagger() registers the Swagger middleware to generate Swagger JSON endpoint while app.UseSwaggerUI() registers the Swagger UI middleware to serve the Swagger UI, which provides a user-friendly interface to explore and test the API endpoints.

```
app.UseHttpsRedirection();
```

This middleware enforces HTTPS by redirecting HTTP requests to HTTPS.

```
app.UseAuthorization();
```

This middleware adds support for authorization. It ensures that the user is authorized to access the resources.

```
app.MapControllers();
```

This line maps the controller actions to endpoints, enabling the routing of HTTP requests to the appropriate controller actions.

```
app.Run();
```

This line runs the application, blocking the calling thread until the host shuts down.

YARP-Specific Configuration

The ASP.NET Core YARP project startup class, Program.cs, has a few extra lines. These are the YARP-specific lines:

```
builder.Services.AddSystemWebAdapters();
```

This method registers System.Web adapters. System web adapters provide middleware to adapt HTTP requests and responses for legacy systems, such as Asp.NET legacy app. The library can be used from both ASP.NET Framework and ASP.NET Core and was written to help developers who have a reliance on System.Web in their legacy project and are looking to migrate.

For example, using HttpContext.Current is something we did a lot in our legacy Konstrukt system; however, the current context is accessed through an abstraction and dependency injection in ASP.NET Core, with the IHttpContextAccessor interface. Unless you've used HttpContext.Current extensively in your project, I highly recommend refactoring the code by abstracting HttpContext access into service classes. By replacing direct calls with abstractions, as well as minimizing HttpContext usage, you ensure cleaner and more maintainable code post-migration with less long-term dependency on adapters.

```
builder.Services.AddHttpForwarder();
```

This registers the HTTP forwarder service required for YARP to forward HTTP requests to other destinations, which are configured in launchSettings.json.

```
app.UseSystemWebAdapters();
```

Adds the middleware for system web adapters into the request pipeline.

```
app.MapForwarder("/{**catch-all}", app.
Configuration["ProxyTo"])
```

Maps a forwarding route that catches all incoming requests and forwards them to the configured destination. This specific line sets up a catch-all route using YARP to forward requests to the URL specified in the configuration (app.Configuration["ProxyTo"]). The path "/{**catch-all}" matches all incoming paths and forwards them to the specified back end.

```
.Add(static builder => ((RouteEndpointBuilder)builder).Order =
int.MaxValue);
```

This adjusts the order of the endpoint to ensure it is evaluated last, ensuring that the forwarder route has the lowest priority and only gets hit if no other routes match the incoming request. This is crucial for catch-all routes to function correctly as a fallback.

Configuration Providers

ASP.NET Core supports a variety of configuration sources and types to effectively manage application settings with something called configuration providers. Configuration providers are components that read configuration data from various sources. By using configuration providers, you can efficiently manage settings in a way that is flexible and scalable. This enables you to seamlessly adjust to different environments or deployment scenarios, all without the need for any code modifications. The framework allows configuration through file-based sources such as JSON, XML, and INI files.

Specifically, JSON files like appsettings.json and environment-specific files such as appsettings.Development.json are commonly used to store settings. Additionally, configuration values can be sourced from environment variables like we did in the console app. Environment variables makes it easy to manage settings in different deployment environments and can be set directly from Visual Studio if you have variables just for development purposes.

Command-line arguments provide another method to pass configuration values when starting the application. This is often used to switch between Dev and QA or Stage environments.

Below are some common types of configuration providers:

Different types of configuration providers:

- Azure Key Vault Configuration Provider: Loads app configuration values from Azure Key Vault secrets.

- Command-Line Configuration Provider: Allows settings to be passed via command-line arguments.

- Environment Variables Configuration Provider: Loads configuration settings from environment variables.

- File Configuration Provider (INI, JSON, XML): Reads configuration data from files.

- Key-Per-File Configuration Provider (Directory files):
  Reads configuration from individual files in a directory,
  often used in containerized environments like Docker.
  The key is the file name while the value is the file's
  contents.

- Memory Configuration Provider (in-memory
  collections): Stores configuration data in memory as
  key-value pairs.

- User Secrets (Secret Manager): Primarily designed
  for local development, allows you to securely store
  sensitive information on your local machine without
  the risk of committing it to your Git repository.

- Custom Configuration Provider: Enables you to create
  your own provider to grab configuration data from any
  custom source

As mentioned earlier, file settings aren't the best or most secure option even if it's just for dev environment. Therefore, for development purposes, sensitive data can be securely managed using the User Secrets manager, while for production, Azure Key Vault can be used to store and access sensitive information securely. You can also use ASP.NET Core custom configuration providers, allowing integration with other configuration sources.

The configuration API in ASP.NET Core is very flexible, supporting binding to primitive types, nullable types, arrays, lists, and complex types, including custom POCO classes. This allows for strong typing and easy access to configuration values throughout the application. Configuration can be accessed using the IConfiguration interface, and values can be bound to POCO classes or registered with the dependency injection container for seamless integration. Let's look at two examples.

Mapping IOptions

We'll create a controller that accepts an IOptions in its constructor, injecting the options retrieved from any of the methods we mentioned earlier.

```
using Microsoft.AspNetCore.Http;
using Microsoft.AspNetCore.Mvc;
using Microsoft.Extensions.Options;

namespace Konstrukt.SL.Main.Core.Controllers {
    [Route("api/[controller]")]
    [ApiController]
    public class WeatherApiSettingsController(IOptions<Weather
    ApiOptions> settings) : ControllerBase
    {
        private readonly WeatherApiOptions _settings = settings
        .Value;

        [HttpGet]
        public IActionResult Get() {
            return Ok(_settings.BaseUrl);
        }
    }
}
```

The WeatherApiOptions class:

```
public class WeatherApiOptions
{
    public string BaseUrl { get; set; }
}
```

We'll add this section in the appsettings file

```
"WeatherApiOptions": {
  "BaseUrl": "https://api.weather.com"
}
```

And a dev url for the BaseUrl in the development JSON

```
"WeatherApiOptions": {
  "BaseUrl": "https://dev.api.weather.com"
}
```

The type mapping is then registered in Program.cs:

```
builder.Services.Configure<WeatherApiOptions>(builder.
Configuration.GetSection(nameof(WeatherApiOptions)));
```

And that's it. If we run the app, still in development (default), we should get the dev BaseUrl for the weather API. If we really wanted to use App.config, or other XML-based config files, we could do so. Konstrukt, for example, encrypted the data in the config files; they were only available behind a VPN and had other protective measures. We did however migrate to using vaults at a later point. Anyway, to use a config file, you add it to the project making sure the Build properties are set to Content and Copy Always.

Register the XML configuration (this requires the Microsoft.Extensions. Configuration.Xml package which should be included from the start).

```
builder.Configuration.AddXmlFile("App.config", optional: true,
reloadOnChange: true);
```

Create the POCO class, and register the POCO options mapping. Inject the options where needed.

```
public class AppConfigOptions {
    public string DbConnection { get; set; }
}
```

// Program.cs

```
builder.Services.Configure<AppConfigOptions>(options => {
    var connectionStringSection = builder.Configuration.
    GetSection("connectionStrings:add:DbConnection");
    options.DbConnection = connectionStringSection
    ["connectionString"];
});
```

    // *WeatherApiSettingsController.cs*

```
[AllowAnonymous]
[Route("api/[controller]")]
[ApiController]
public class WeatherApiSettingsController(IOptions<Weather
ApiOptions> apiSettings, IOptions<AppConfigOptions>
appConfigOptions) : ControllerBase
{
    private readonly WeatherApiOptions _weatherApiOptions
    = apiSettings.Value;
    private readonly AppConfigOptions _appConfigOptions
    = appConfigOptions.Value;

    [HttpGet]
    public IActionResult Get()
    {
        var db = _appConfigOptions.DbConnection;

        return Ok(_weatherApiOptions.BaseUrl);
    }
}
```

If the Options POCO class doesn't contain the options, you can set a breakpoint in the Program.cs class, and using the debugger, look at the sections the builder.Configuration has. Each section has a FullPath, which is the one we want to double check (Figure 6-11).

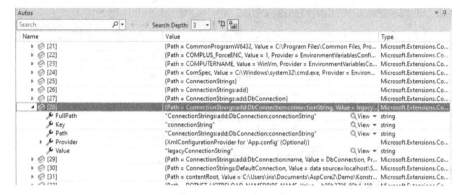

Figure 6-11. *Using the Autos window and a breakpoint in the builder can help you troubleshoot missing configurations*

In ASP.NET Core, the order in which configuration sources are added determines their priority. Configuration providers that are added later can override the values from earlier ones. This allows for a flexible configuration where you can specify defaults in a JSON file and override them with environment variables or command-line arguments. Generally, you want the following order: Files, Environment Variables, Console.

Configuring a Custom DI Container

We use Autofac for Dependency Injection (DI), and although the Microsoft built-in dependency injection is fantastic, we want to speed up the migration by using our Autofac wiring for now. Autofac provides advanced capabilities like property injection, dynamic module loading, and more flexible registration options, but the trade-off is complexity and overhead, especially in simpler projects. Although we made plans to migrate to built-in DI at a later point, we chose to use Autofac for the time being. Using Autofac is as simple as installing the Autofac extensions package Autofac.Extensions.DependencyInjection, moving over our IoC folder which contains our module (where all our types have been registered, most of them mapping to an interface). Registering your own DI container is easily configured through the host:

```
builder.Host.UseServiceProviderFactory(new
AutofacServiceProviderFactory());
builder.Host.ConfigureContainer<ContainerBuilder>(cb =>
{
    cb.RegisterModule(new MainModule());
});
```

At this point we can run the ASP.NET Core YARP project and test the controller we migrated.

ASP.NET Core HttpContext

A noticeable change from ASP.NET Framework to ASP.NET Core is how we access the HttpContext. In ASP.NET Core, we can't reference it directly unless we use System.WebAdapters. But as I said earlier, if it's not too much trouble, use a layer of abstraction. We got in the habit of passing around the HTTP context in our libraries. This resulted in strong dependencies and caused additional problems when working with multiple threads and losing the original thread context. The layer of abstraction makes testing easier, and the scoping is clearer.

Konstrukt.Shared uses HttpContext.Current in its CurrentRequest type. We'll use the Upgrade Assistant and migrate it to .NET Standard 2.0 before we make some changes to our CurrentRequest type.

To facilitate this, it's beneficial to introduce a layer of abstraction. By abstracting the direct dependency on HttpContext.Current, you create a more modular and testable architecture. Let's walk through this process step by step.

Step 1: Create an Abstraction Interface

The first step is to define an interface that abstracts the methods and properties of HttpContext that your application relies on. For example:

```
public interface IRequest
{
    NameValueCollection Headers();
    string HttpMethod { get; }
}
```

This interface represents the methods and properties we need from HttpContext. By depending on this interface rather than the concrete HttpContext class, we can easily swap out implementations, making our code more flexible and easier to test.

Step 2: Implement the Interface in the Legacy System

In the legacy system, we can implement this interface by wrapping the existing HttpContext.Current:

```
public class SlimRequest : IRequest {
    public NameValueCollection Headers() => HttpContext.
        Current.Request.Headers;
    public string HttpMethod => HttpContext.Current.Request.
        HttpMethod;
}
```

Here, SlimRequest acts as an adapter, translating calls to IRequest methods into the corresponding HttpContext.Current calls.

Step 3: Implement the Interface in ASP.NET Core

In the new ASP.NET Core project, you implement the same interface using IHttpContextAccessor:

```
public class SlimRequest : IRequest
{
    private readonly IHttpContextAccessor _httpContextAccessor;

    public SlimRequest(IHttpContextAccessor httpContext
    Accessor)
    {
        _httpContextAccessor = httpContextAccessor;
    }

    public NameValueCollection Headers()
    {
        var collection = new NameValueCollection();
        foreach (var item in _httpContextAccessor.HttpContext.
        Request.Headers)
        {
            collection.Add(item.Key, item.Value);
        }
        return collection;
    }

    public string HttpMethod => _httpContextAccessor.
    HttpContext.Request.Method;
}
```

This implementation uses IHttpContextAccessor to access the HttpContext in ASP.NET Core, ensuring that the new system remains compatible with the abstraction.

Step 4: Update Dependent Classes

Next, you update classes that previously depended on HttpContext.Current to use the new IRequest interface instead. For example, consider the CurrentRequest class:

```
public class CurrentRequest : ICurrentRequest
{
    private readonly IRequest _request;

    public CurrentRequest(IRequest request)
    {
        _request = request;
    }

    // Other properties and methods using _request instead of
        HttpContext.Current
}
```

By injecting IRequest into CurrentRequest, you make this class independent of the specific implementation of HttpContext, allowing it to work seamlessly in both the legacy and ASP.NET Core environments.

Step 5: Register the Implementations

Finally, you register the appropriate implementations in the DI container based on the environment:

```
// ASP.NET Core
builder.Services.AddSingleton<IHttpContextAccessor,
HttpContextAccessor>();
builder.Services.AddSingleton<IRequest, SlimRequest>();

// Legacy ASP.NET
builder.RegisterType<SlimRequest>().As<IRequest>();
```

At this point we could check if we can remove the System.WebAdapters by using Find Dependent Code. Similar to what we discussed earlier in the book, you can right-click the package and then select "Find Dependent Code." There is one more class using the HttpContext:

```
public class LoggedInUserRetriever : ILoggedInUserRetriever
{
    public string GetLoggedInUserId() => System.Web.Http
    Context.Current.User.Identity.Name;
}
```

We can refactor to this:

```
using System.Security.Principal;
namespace Konstrukt.Shared
{
    public class LoggedInUserRetriever : ILoggedInUser
    Retriever {
        private readonly IPrincipal _principal;

        public LoggedInUserRetriever(IPrincipal principal)
        => _principal = principal;

        public string GetLoggedInUserId() {
            IIdentity userNameClaim = _principal.Identity;

            return userNameClaim.Name;
        }
    }
}
```

The more abstractions we have, the easier it's going to be to do an incremental upgrade. We can even add a layer of abstraction for our DriveInfoHelper, by using System.IO.Abstractions and other abstraction libraries. Not only does this help us inject different implementations depending on platform, but it also makes testing easier, which we investigate later. But first, let's talk middleware.

ASP.NET Core Middleware

Although the ASP.NET Core project runs without errors, we still have a problem. It doesn't support multitenancy and uses the default database connection that we set up earlier. To address this, we will modify the request pipeline to capture the subdomain from each incoming request, verify its authorization, and handle it accordingly. This will be done by using middleware. If you have previous experience with Owin, this should feel familiar.

In an application pipeline, middleware is a code segment responsible for handling requests and responses. The middleware segments, or components as they are often referred to as, are assembled into an application pipeline, where each component can either process the incoming request and pass it to the next component in the pipeline or handle the response. Common uses of middleware include handling authentication, logging, and error handling. In our old project, we used the MultiTenancyHandler.UseTenantContext(IDataStoreContext). We'll create a TenantMiddleware that uses the method mentioned above:

```
public class TenantMiddleware(RequestDelegate next)
{
    public async Task InvokeAsync(HttpContext context,
    IMultiTenancyHandler multiTenancyHandler, IDataStoreContext
    dataStoreContext) {
        multiTenancyHandler.UseTenantContext(dataStoreContext);
        // Call the next middleware in the pipeline
        await next(context);
    }
}
```

This is a very naïve implementation meant to give you an idea how the flow can be configured and how middleware is created and registered. Remember this is a pipeline, so it does matter where in the pipeline you register the middleware.

118

The middleware is then added to the pipeline:

```
// Middleware to handle multitenancy
app.UseMiddleware<TenantMiddleware>();
```

I added a second tenant database by scripting the schema and exported the objects (with some modifications so we can differentiate between the two tenants) and could confirm that the multitenancy logic worked.

Enabling CORS

Enabling Cross-Origin Resource Sharing (CORS) in an ASP.NET Core application can be done with relative ease by adding a CORS middleware. Add the following NuGet package to the project:

```
dotnet add package Microsoft.AspNetCore.Cors
```

Configuring CORS in Startup.cs

```
var corsPolicyName = "MyAllowSpecificOrigins";
builder.Services.AddCors(options =>
{
    options.AddPolicy(name: "MyAllowSpecificOrigins",
        policy => {
            policy.WithOrigins("http://example.com",
                "http://www.contoso.com");
        });
});
```

And after App.UseRouting() (if you have this line in your Program.cs), but before app.UseAuthentication:

```
// Option 1: Apply the CORS policy globally to all endpoints
app.UseCors(corsPolicyName);
```

```
// Option 2: Apply the CORS policy only to specific endpoints
   that have [EnableCors("MyAllowSpecificOrigins")]
// app.UseCors();
```

You can also use endpoint routing by adding this after the app.
UseCors() call (notice policy is not passed in as a parameter).

```
app.UseEndpoints(endpoints =>
{
    endpoints.MapGet("/echo",
        context => context.Response.WriteAsync("echo"))
        .RequireCors(MyAllowSpecificOrigins);

    endpoints.MapControllers()
            .RequireCors(MyAllowSpecificOrigins);
});
```

By using endpoint routing and the RequireCors extension, you have
the ability to set specific policies for particular endpoints. Endpoint routing
in ASP.NET Core is a feature that allows you to configure request handling
for your application in a more granular and flexible way. Endpoints can be
controllers, Blazor, razor pages, SignalR, gRPC, and more. It provides a way
to map incoming requests to route handlers (endpoints) and allows you to
apply middleware, such as CORS policies, at a per-endpoint level. I'll get
back to policies later.

```
app.UseEndpoints(endpoints => {
    // Apply CORS policy to specific endpoints
    endpoints.MapGet("/api/corstest",
            context => context.Response.WriteAsync("hello"))
        .RequireCors(corsPolicyName);
// Add more here
});
```

Unit and Integration Tests

It's been a long time since we last talked about tests, and now that we've begun migrating the controllers, it's necessary for us to focus on the tests. We have three options:

1. Ignore the tests during the migration.

2. Use conditional compilation and multiple targets in the test projects.

3. Use separate test projects and add to the new test projects as we migrate more classes and controllers.

You may be curious about why I included the first option. Well, if you are planning to migrate the solution all at once and it's a small and easily transferable system, then this option could be feasible. However, for most solutions its either option two or three. And as I shared earlier, conditional compilation can be a pain and adds unnecessary complexity. That leaves us with the last option, using a separate test project(s). We've already migrated Konstrukt.BL.Main and its dependencies, so we can migrate to a new project by using the Upgrade Assistant. The shared test library, containing mock helpers and other utility classes, was migrated to .NET Standard 2.0, and the Konstrukt.BL.Main.Test to Konstrukt.BL.Main. Core.Test targeting .NET 8. If the test runner is not detecting the new tests, you should verify the project properties and type, and update the NuGet packages.

JWT Token Authentication

Although we haven't delved into authentication and authorization much, it's important to discuss it as we migrate more controllers. Konstrukt uses an authentication service which for security reasons isn't added to the demo. However, let's pretend we are using JWT authentication. I've added

JWT token authorization to all our controllers in Konstrukt.SL.Main and an endpoint to generate a JWT token that is for demo purposes only. All our requests, except the public controller, require a JWT token now. Controllers that haven't been migrated will be routed using YARP and therefore will require the JWT token. However, the controller we migrated does not require authorization. This makes sense, as the ASP.NET Core YARP app doesn't have any authorization requirements for its own controllers.

When incrementally migrating an ASP.NET Framework application to ASP.NET Core, particularly in terms of handling JWT (JSON Web Token) authentication, we need to ensure a seamless integration of authentication mechanisms across both platforms, and we can do this by setting up JWT authentication in the ASP.NET Core application to validate the same tokens issued by the ASP.NET Framework application. If you use a third party, then the flow will differ, but the takeaway is that you need to set up the same token configuration for both services. Let's make sure both applications share the same JWT configuration (secret key, issuer, and audience) by moving out the JWT token parameters code to the Konstrukt. Shared library. In the demo app, this has been hardcoded for demo purposes; do not hardcode the configuration values and keys!

```
builder.Services.AddAuthentication(x =>
    {
        x.DefaultAuthenticateScheme = JwtBearerDefaults.
                                    AuthenticationScheme;
        x.DefaultChallengeScheme = JwtBearerDefaults.
                                    AuthenticationScheme;
    })
    .AddJwtBearer(x =>
    {
        x.SaveToken = true;
```

```
        x.TokenValidationParameters = JwtToken.CreateToken
                                            ValidationParameters();
    });

builder.Services.AddAuthorization(options => {
    options.FallbackPolicy = new AuthorizationPolicyBuilder()
        .AddAuthenticationSchemes(JwtBearerDefaults.
        AuthenticationScheme)
        .RequireAuthenticatedUser()
        .Build();
});
...
app.UseAuthentication();
app.UseAuthorization();
```

As you can see in the code, I've also added a FallbackPolicy. ASP.NET
Core policies are like a set of rules you create to control who can access
different parts of your app. Think of them as a way to define what a user
needs to have or be able to do to get into certain sections or perform
certain tasks. Policy-based authorization is configured in Program.cs,
and you can apply them to the entire service, just specific controllers, or
even individual requests. A fallback policy like the one I added makes sure
that even controllers without [Authorize] attribute require authorization,
unless explicitly overridden by [AllowAnonymous].

ASP.NET Core Identity

ASP.NET Core Identity While there are some similarities between ASP.
NET Identity and ASP.NET Core Identity, there are also significant
differences that require additional work when migrating. You will need
to migrate to the new schema, which includes new tables and columns.
Importantly, the password criteria and hashing algorithms have changed.

For example, here is the same password hashed using ASP.NET Identity:

AOstUiMCRZkeV7mQqj4ZygJGtZuKQXxp9Ir+5vQQBikFfGScUcCVYks/
N9E/5zC9Xg==

And hashed in ASP.NET Core Identity:

AQAAAAEAACcQAAAAEAYCHwW5NfOnVU84CAhX7xnMEDrXTqq6XO/d7kIv1+HTlcP
felFEgu5mtKEq+LT61A==

Microsoft recommends leaving the password empty after migrating the users to the new schema and prompting users to change their passwords.

The list below shows a high-level comparison of the Identity tables created with ASP.NET and ASP.NET Core. There are differences even at the column level.

- **ASP.NET Identity Tables**

  - AspNetRoles

  - AspNetUserClaims

  - AspNetUserLogins

  - AspNetUserRoles

  - AspNetUsers

- **ASP.NET Core Identity Tables**

  - AspNetRoleClaims

  - AspNetRoles

  - AspNetUserClaims

  - AspNetUserLogins

  - AspNetUserRoles

  - AspNetUsers

  - AspNetUserTokens

Migrating from ASP.NET Identity to ASP.NET Core Identity involves several steps, but there's no one-size-fits-all tool that handles everything for you. However, you can use Entity Framework Core's migration capabilities alongside custom scripts to aid in the process.

Migrating to the New Schema

These are the steps for migrating to the new schema:
Install Necessary NuGet Packages:

- Microsoft.AspNetCore.Identity.EntityFrameworkCore

- Microsoft.EntityFrameworkCore.SqlServer

Configure Identity in Startup.cs or Program.cs:

```
builder.Services.AddDbContext<ApplicationDbContext>(options =>
    options.UseSqlServer(builder.Configuration.GetConnection
    String("DefaultConnection")));
builder.Services.AddIdentity<ApplicationUser, IdentityRole>()
    .AddEntityFrameworkStores<ApplicationDbContext>()
    .AddDefaultTokenProviders();

builder.Services.Configure<IdentityOptions>(options =>
{
    options.Password.RequireDigit = true;
    options.Password.RequiredLength = 8;
    options.Password.RequireNonAlphanumeric = false;
    options.Password.RequireUppercase = true;
    options.Password.RequireLowercase = false;
});
```

Important note: These settings are configured to match the older password requirements from the legacy system, allowing users to continue using their existing passwords. While this approach ensures a smoother transition during the migration, it's advisable to prompt the user to set a new password, using the new and stronger requirements.

The next step in this implementation is to define Identity Models and DbContext (I added the models in Konstrukt.Entities.Core):

```
public class ApplicationUser : IdentityUser
{
    // Additional properties can go here
}

public class ApplicationDbContext : IdentityDbContext<Applic
ationUser>
{
    public ApplicationDbContext(DbContextOptions<Application
    DbContext> options)
        : base(options)
    {
    }
}
```

Create and apply migrations by running the following command in the NuGet Console:

```
Update-Database
```

You might have to specify EF tools if you have both EF 6 and EF 8 and up. In the demo code, I've also used two separate database contexts and therefore had to specify the database context.

```
EntityFrameworkCore\Update-Database -Context Konstrukt.
Entities.Core.ApplicationDbContext
```

Finally, use scripts to export and import the data into the new ASP.NET Core Identity tables. Ensure that you handle passwords correctly (consider prompting users to reset their passwords).

You can find the AuthController in the example source code, as well as the Postman script to generate a JWT token based on user login.

If I remember correctly, it took us about half a day to migrate the users to the new schema. Our authentication was entirely handled by our independent authentication service, although there was the possibility of utilizing the ASP.NET Core YARP service if our authentication had been a part of that project. We would then have authenticated the user and generated a JWT token like we did earlier. Integrating ASP.NET Core Identity with JWT (JSON Web Tokens) is a common approach for securing web APIs.

Summary

In this chapter, we dove into the incremental migration of our ASP.NET service using YARP. We kicked things off by setting up a new ASP.NET Core Web API project to run alongside the legacy app, thanks to YARP's reverse proxy magic. This approach allowed us to migrate controllers one at a time without rushing.

We walked through the YARP project setup, configured multiple startup projects, and used the Upgrade Assistant to migrate controllers, starting with the simplest ones. This step-by-step migration ensured that dependencies were resolved gradually, making the process smoother.

We also took a closer look at the ASP.NET Core project structure, highlighting key components like Program.cs, appsettings.json, and middleware for multitenancy and CORS. Using Autofac for dependency injection helped us keep things familiar while speeding up the migration.

We've also talked about testing and created separate test projects to avoid the headaches of conditional compilation. We wrapped up by discussing JWT token authentication and ASP.NET Core Identity schema changes.

Next chapter, we'll finish migrating the remaining controllers, clean up the solution, and refactor everything to Minimal APIs and gRPC.

CHAPTER 7

Migration Part 3: Cleaning Up

We have successfully overcome all the main obstacles related to migration, and I've migrated the remaining controllers using the Upgrade option, similar to what we did with the initial controller, the AccessController. After confirming the tests run green and all the endpoints work, we can continue with additional cleanup.

The ASP.NET Core YARP project is now our only Konstrukt.SL.Main project moving forward. We simply remove the reverse proxy and routing to the old Konstrukt.SL.Main, as well as the old ASP.NET app and dependencies that aren't used by other libraries.

Removing YARP

With all the controllers migrated over, we don't need YARP anymore, which means we can remove it. We can always add it back if we find usage for it, but I like to keep my projects clean and without unnecessary code. Removing YARP is easy.

In Program.cs we can remove the following lines:

```
builder.Services.AddHttpForwarder();
...
app.MapForwarder("/{**catch-all}", app.
```

© Iris Classon 2024
I. Classon, *Migrating ASP.NET Microservices to ASP.NET Core 8*,
https://doi.org/10.1007/979-8-8688-1026-8_7

```
Configuration["ProxyTo"])
    .Add(static builder => ((RouteEndpointBuilder)builder).
    Order = int.MaxValue);
```

By removing these lines, you are effectively disabling the proxy behavior, meaning all requests will now be handled directly by the ASP. NET Core project. This change assumes that all required endpoints have been fully migrated and are functioning correctly in the new environment, allowing you to safely remove the reverse proxy without disrupting the application. We can then remove the YARP.ReverseProxy package (Figure 7-1).

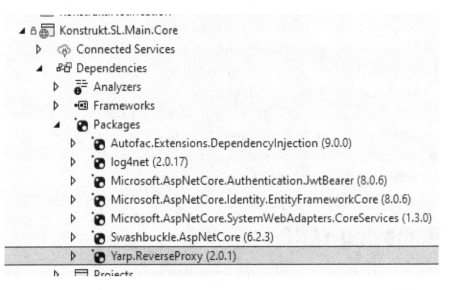

Figure 7-1. *YARP is installed as a single package and is easy to uninstall*

Finally, we can clean up any associated configuration settings, such as the ProxyTo environment variable in launchSettings.json.:

```
"ProxyTo": http://localhost:52637
```
Moreover, we can remove the configuration for launching the other application.

130

```
"IIS Express": {
  "commandName": "IISExpress",
  "launchBrowser": true,
  "environmentVariables": {
    "ASPNETCORE_ENVIRONMENT": "Development",
    "ProxyTo": "http://localhost:52637"
    "ASPNETCORE_ENVIRONMENT": "Development"
  }
}
```

We will also make sure to set the ASP.NET Core project as the startup project instead of multiple startup projects, before removing the old app and its dependencies that haven't been migrated in-place, as well as the test projects targeting .NET 4.8. Keep in mind that removing projects, files, and folders in Visual Studio doesn't necessarily remove them completely from the solution directory. Open the solution folder in Explorer, and manually delete them there as well. You can see the before (Figure 7-2) and after (Figure 7-3) below.

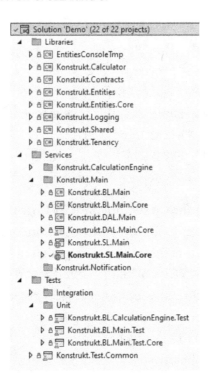

Figure 7-2. *The solution before the cleanup*

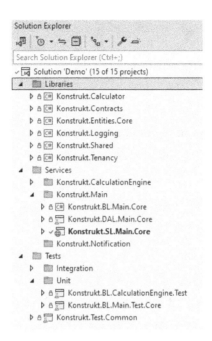

Figure 7-3. *The solution after the cleanup*

Do a final check and make sure the namespaces correlate to their path and project and fix any leftover Warnings in the Error List.

ASP.NET Core Features: Minimal APIs

The migration is complete, yet there is one more thing I'd like to do. In the book's opening section, we explored the benefits of migration, and one of the positive aspects mentioned was the addition of new features. Our controllers are clean and straightforward and good candidates for Minimal APIs. Minimal APIs are a streamlined way to build small, focused HTTP APIs in ASP.NET Core. Boilerplate code has been abstracted away leaving us with small, yet equally powerful, endpoints ideal for lightweight APIs that are perfect for microservices.

Example:

```
app.MapGet("/api/helloauth/", () => Results.Ok("Helloauth")).
RequireAuthorization();
```

Defining routes and handlers directly in the Program.cs file removes the need for separate controller classes.

Minimal APIs are a good fit for microservices and simple APIs and for prototyping.

The AccessController, for example, could be refactored to a Minimal API registration.

```
[ApiController]
[Route("api/Main")]
public class AccessController : ControllerBase {
    private readonly IAccessGroupRetriver _accessGroupRetriver;

    public AccessController(IAccessGroupRetriver accessGroup
    Retriver) => _accessGroupRetriver = accessGroupRetriver;

    [Authorize]
    [HttpGet()]
    [Route("~/api/Main/access/apps/{appId}")]
    public IActionResult Get(string appId) => Ok(_accessGroup
    Retriver.GetAccessGroup(appId));
}
```

As a Minimal API:

```
app.MapGet("/api/Main/access/apps/{appId}",
    (string appId, IAccessGroupRetriver accessGroup
    Retriever) =>
        Results.Ok(accessGroupRetriever.GetAccessGroup(appId)))
        .RequireAuthorization();
```

Endpoint Explorer

At the beginning of our incremental migration, I mentioned that Endpoint Explorer was a powerful feature. Let's have a look!

We can test the endpoints using Endpoints Explorer in Visual Studio. Select the following in the main menu: View ➤ Other Windows ➤ Endpoint Explorer as shown in Figure 7-4.

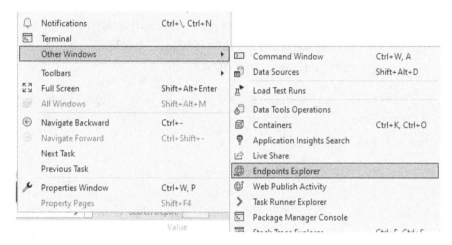

Figure 7-4. *Endpoint Explorer is a Visual Studio feature found under Other Windows*

Endpoint Explorer lists the endpoints, including the Minimal APIs endpoints. We can right-click any endpoint and generate a request (Figure 7-5).

Figure 7-5. *Generating a request is done by right-click ➤ Generate Request*

This creates a .http file with the request, and the file can be saved and reused. You can add headers to the requests for authorization, and see the output in a separate window (Figure 7-6).

```
@Konstrukt.SL.Main.Core_HostAddress = https://localhost:7056
@appId = 07054ace-86f5-4f7a-9e14-8bed3c552cd0
@token = Bearer eyJhbGciOiJIUzI1NiIsInR5cCI6IkpXVCJ9.eyJ
        1bmlxdWVfbmFtZSI6InRlc3R1c2VyIiwibmJmIjoxNzE4NjQ1Mz
        YxLCJleHAiOjE3MTg2NDg5NjEsImlhdCI6MTcxODY4NTM2MSwia
        XNzIjoieW91cklzc3VlciIsImF1ZCI6InlvdXJBdWRpZW5jZSJ9
        .2zLzJmgYpAHppT32GD1gfTQorJLvgcLZz11Mh4BHHsU
```

```
GET {{Konstrukt.SL.Main.Core_HostAddress}}/api/Main/access/
apps/{{appId}}
Authorization: {{token}}
```

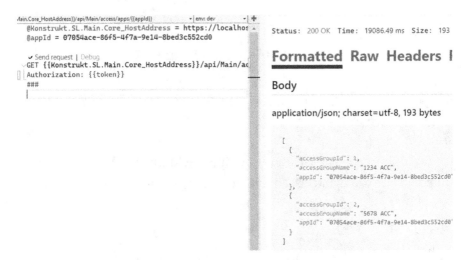

Figure 7-6. *The Request result is shown in a separate window*

Http Environment Files

Checking in a token, secrets, or passwords, is not something you want to do, but you would want to check in the .http file. There are a few ways to deal with this, by using a key vault, or environment files with specific user files that are not checked in. If you create a http-env.json file with the non-sensitive data, you can then create a similar file but with .user added to the extension and add your own personal configuration.

http-env.json file:

```
{
  "dev": {
    "token": ""
  }
}
```

http-env.json.user file:

```
{
  "dev": {
    "token": "testtoken"
  }
}
```

If the token fails to update after making changes in the .user file, try closing and opening Visual Studio again. I will proceed to convert the remaining controllers into Minimal APIs, with some of them needing more adjustment.

Complex Types

Complex types need to be explicitly bound from the request body. You need to use the [FromBody] attribute to specify that the parameter should be bound from the body of the request. For simple types (e.g., int, string), parameters can be automatically bound from route or query string. Complex types are bound like this:

```
public class UserInfo
{
    public string FirstName { get; set; }
    public string LastName { get; set; }
    public int Age { get; set; }
}
[HttpPost] public IActionResult CreateUser([FromBody] UserInfo
userInfo) { return Ok(); }
```

Simple types are bound from the route or query string:

```
[HttpGet("user/{id}")] public IActionResult GetUser(int id) {
return Ok(); }
```

Resolving Services

The [FromServices] attribute explicitly tells the minimal API to resolve the parameter from the dependency injection container instead of inferring it from the request body. For example, the ILogger parameter is marked with [FromServices] to ensure it is correctly injected from the services.

Optional Parameters

In Minimal APIs, parameters declared in route handlers are by default required. This means that if a request matches the route, the route handler will only execute if all required parameters are provided. If any required parameter is missing, the framework will return an error indicating that the request is invalid. Use a nullable type or declare a default value for optional parameters.

```
app.MapGet("/items/{number?}", (int? number)...
// or
app.MapGet("/items/{number?}", (int number = 1)...
```

Special Types

Certain types in Minimal APIs are automatically bound without the need for explicit attributes:

- HttpContext

- HttpRequest and HttpResponse

- CancellationToken

- ClaimsPrincipal

File Uploads

File uploads can be done using IFormFile and IformFileCollection attributes.

Return Types

There are several types of responses that you can return; here is a list of some of the supported types:

- JSON: You can return JSON objects directly using the Results.Json method.

- Plain text: For simple text responses, use the Results. Text method.

- Status codes: Return specific HTTP status codes using methods like Results.StatusCode, Results.BadRequest, and Results.NotFound.

- Stream: Stream large amounts of data directly from the endpoint.

- File: Serve files from the server using the Results. File method.

- Redirect: Redirect requests to another URL using Results.Redirect, facilitating URL forwarding or permanent redirections.

- Custom result types: Implement custom result types by creating a class that implements the IResult interface.

Organizing Minimal APIs Endpoints

Minimal APIs are powerful, and for us a perfect fit. However, you may have noticed that as I added the remaining controller requests to Program. cs, the class grew considerably which made it harder to read. Generally I prefer smaller classes with specific responsibility, and although program.

cs is a bootstrapper which means it does different types of configurations and setup, we can still clean up the API registrations. For example, I could declare the routes in a separate extension method(s) like this:

```
public static class ApiEndpoints {
    public static void MapAccessEndpoints(this IEndpoint
    RouteBuilder routes) {
        routes.MapGet("/api/Main/access/apps/{appId}",
            (string appId, IAccessGroupRetriver accessGroup
            Retriever) =>
                Results.Ok(accessGroupRetriever.GetAccessGroup
                (appId))).RequireAuthorization();
        // Add more endpoints as needed
    }

    public static void MapOtherEndpoints(this IEndpointRoute
    Builder routes) {
        routes.MapGet("/api/other/{id}",
            (string id) => Results.Ok($"Other {id}"));
        // Add more endpoints as needed
    }
}
```

And use them by a calling the extension methods from Program.cs:

```
app.MapAccessEndpoints();
app.MapOtherEndpoints();
```

See the source code for the full example.

Using the Built-in ILogger

Logging only got an honorable mention earlier in the book, but I'd like to take a closer look.

ASP.NET Core has made logging a priority; it is after all important for monitoring application behavior, diagnosing issues, and understanding the application's runtime dynamics when things go wrong, and right.

Logging in ASP.NET Core is integrated into the framework and configured similarly to other configuration objects and accessed through dependency injection. We have several logging providers to choose between:

Built-in logging providers

- Console: Logs to the console window.

- Debug: Logs to the debug output window.

- EventSource: Logs to EventSource, starting from ASP. NET Core 2.2, for event tracing.

- EventLog: Logs to the Windows Event Log.

Third-party logging providers

- NLog

- Serilog

- log4net

- Microsoft.Extensions.Logging.AzureAppServices

- And many more

Configuring Logging in ASP.NET Core

Logging providers are configured in the ConfigureLogging method. By default, ASP.NET Core includes Console, Debug, and EventSource logging providers. To add third-party providers like NLog or lof4net, you typically use their respective extension methods to integrate them into the logging pipeline. We've used log4net, but decided to switch to NLog, but keep the logging pattern as is.

Configuring for NLog

Configuring third-party logging providers differs depending on the provider, but most of them have a package that has extension methods for registering the logging provider and a configuration file or object. Once configured, the logger is accessed by injecting the ILogger<T>. NLog Nuget dependencies are added to the project in the csproj file, by using a specific version or floating versions. A floating version allows flexibility by automatically using the latest version within a specified range. This is achieved by using a wildcard character (*) in the version number.

We added the following NLog NuGet dependencies to our project:

```
<PackageReference Include="NLog.Web.AspNetCore" Version="*" />
<PackageReference Include="NLog" Version="*" />
```

An nlog.config was added to the project with its Build Action set to Content and Copy to Output Directory set to Copy always. This file contains configuration information, logging patterns, and the connection string. Since we don't want to check in the connection string into source control and risk sharing sensitive information, we can grab it from environment variables or a secure configuration store like we discussed earlier.

Enabling NLog in Program.cs:

```
var logger = LogManager.Setup().
LoadConfigurationFromFile("nlog.config").
GetCurrentClassLogger();
builder.Logging.ClearProviders();
builder.Logging.SetMinimumLevel(Microsoft.Extensions.Logging.
LogLevel.Debug);
builder.Host.UseNLog();
```

Using the ILogger:

```
public static void MapLogEndpoints(this IEndpointRoute
Builder routes) {
    routes.MapGet("/api/Log",
        ([FromServices] ILogger<IEndpointRouteBuilder>
        logger) => {
            logger.Log(LogLevel.Information, "Log called");
            return Results.Ok();
        }).AllowAnonymous();

    routes.MapGet("/api/Throw",
            () => { throw new System.Exception("Exception
            thrown"); })
        .AllowAnonymous();
}
```

Native AOT

Enabling Native AOT (Ahead-of-Time) compilation in an ASP.NET Core project compiles the application directly to native machine code before it is run, improving performance and reducing startup time. This process produces smaller, self-contained executables. However, certain .NET features like reflection and dynamic code generation may have limitations, so please refer to the Microsoft Documentation to verify that you can use AOT:

https://learn.microsoft.com/en-us/dotnet/core/deploying/
native-aot/

I'll soon walk you through setting up a gRPC service, and the Create New Project dialogue has an Enable AOT publish option (Figure 7-7) which several project types have (including ASP.NET Core).

ASP.NET Core gRPC Service

Framework ⓘ

.NET 8.0 (Long Term Support)

☐ Enable Docker ⓘ

Docker OS ⓘ

Linux

☐ Do not use top-level statements ⓘ

✓ Enable native AOT publish ⓘ

Figure 7-7. *Many newer templates come with the Enable native AOT option, which can also be configured in the project file at a later point*

GRPC

As stated in the book's introduction, Konstrukt encountered issues with performance and memory consumption as a result of extensive calculations and a large amount of data. The Konstruk SaaS system started as a group of Web API microservices loosely based on the REST model, but that doesn't mean we can't change this. ASP .NET Core has support for gRPC (gRPC Remote Procedure Call) which makes it easy to set up a gRPC service. gRPC is an open source framework developed by Google that enables remote procedure calls between client and server applications. It uses HTTP/2 for transport, Protocol Buffers for interface description, and has additional features such as authentication, load balancing, and more. But most importantly for Konstrukt, gRPC is designed for high performance and efficiency. It's highly performant due to its use of HTTP/2, which offers multiplexing, header compression, and a binary

145

protocol for efficient data transmission. It's not new, but the ASP .NET Core gRPC templates make it easier to set up, even for those of us who aren't familiar with it.

Teams might opt for gRPC in a migration process for several key reasons:

- Performance: gRPC provides lower latency and efficiently handles high request volumes with minimal overhead.

- Cross-language integration: Its support for multiple programming languages simplifies the integration of services written in different languages.

- Streaming capabilities: gRPC natively supports bi-directional streaming, which can be more difficult to implement with REST APIs.

- Consistency: It ensures client-server consistency by enforcing strict contracts through Protocol Buffers.

For us specifically, we already had plans to migrate a calculation engine, and with the help of the provided templates and our straightforward code, the resource cost is low, but the potential gains are significant. Walking you through a detailed tutorial on creating and using a gRPC service is beyond the scope of this book, but a good start would be to create a gRPC service using the ASP.NET Core gRPC Service (Figure 7-8) which comes with an example. Microsoft Learn walks you through the basics using the template, as well as setting up a client to consume the service. Read more here: `https://learn.microsoft.com/en-us/aspnet/core/grpc/`. We will however take a quick look. Let's start by creating a new ASP.NET Core gRPC service (Figure 7-8).

| grpc | ✕ | ▾ |

Clear

All languages   ▾   All platforms   ▾   API

No exact matches found

Other results based on your search

gRPC   ASP.NET Core gRPC Service
A project template for creating a gRPC service using ASP.NET Core, with optional support for publishing as native AOT.

| C# | Linux | macOS | Windows | Cloud | Service | Web |

Figure 7-8. *Visual Studio has a template for an ASP.NET Core gRPC service which comes with a simple server example*

Tip   When setting up the gRPC service and running it for the first time, Visual Studio should prompt you to trust the SSL certificate generated. Select yes. If you don't get the option to trust the certificate, and get an SSL error, open the developer command line from the Tools menu in Visual Studio and run the following:

```
dotnet dev-certs https –trust
```

The consuming client I created was a console app, but you could use an ASP.NET Core app as well (or other application types). Here are the general steps for setting up a server and a client. The steps are simplified and only to give you an idea of the workflow.

Creating a gRPC Server

These are the steps for creating a simple server. Although it may appear complex at first, with a bit of practice, you'll become proficient. Naming is a critical aspect to pay close attention to, as it's easy to confuse namespaces. Additionally, be cautious when configuring files to ensure they are correctly set up for either the client or the server.

1. Create gRPC project using the "gRPC Service" template.

2. Define a .proto file in the Protos folder, and define the service and message in the file.

```
syntax = "proto3";

option csharp_namespace = "Konstrukt.Calculation
Engine.Grpc.Server.Protos";

service BudgetForecast {
  rpc CalculateBudgetForecast (BudgetForecastRequest)
  returns (BudgetForecastResponse);
}

message BudgetForecastRequest {
  repeated int32 historical_years = 1;
  repeated Variable variables = 2;
}

message Variable {
  string name = 1;
  double value = 2;
}

message YearlyForecast {
  int32 year = 1;
```

```
    double predicted_budget = 2;
}

message BudgetForecastResponse {
  repeated YearlyForecast forecasts = 1;
}
```

3. Update project f to include the file, and build the project.

```
<ItemGroup>
  <Protobuf Include="Protos\forecast.proto"
  GrpcServices="Server" />
</ItemGroup>
```

4. Implement the service in a new class derived from the generated base class.

```
public class BudgetForecastService : BudgetForecast.
BudgetForecastBase
{
    public override Task<BudgetForecastResponse>
    CalculateBudgetForecast(BudgetForecastRequest
    request, ServerCallContext context)
    {
        var response = new BudgetForecastResponse();

        foreach (var year in request.HistoricalYears)
        {
            double predictedBudget = year * 1000;
            foreach (var variable in request.Variables)
            {
                predictedBudget += variable.Value;
            }
```

```
                    response.Forecasts.Add(new YearlyForecast {
                    Year = year, PredictedBudget = predicted
                    Budget });
              }

              return Task.FromResult(response);
        }
    }
```

5. Configure gRPC in Program.cs and make sure the service is registered and configured.

```
var builder = WebApplication.CreateBuilder(args);

builder.Services.AddGrpc();

var app = builder.Build();

app.MapGrpcService<BudgetForecastService>();
app.MapGet("/", () => "gRPC service is running.");

app.Run();
```

Creating a gRPC Client

These are the steps for creating a client that will communicate with the server:

1. Create console app (or other app).

2. Add the following NuGet packages:

```
Grpc.Net.Client
Google.Protobuf
Grpc.Tools.
```

3. Create a Protos folder, and add the same proto file as earlier, but use the client namespace.

4. Include .proto file in the project file like we did above, making sure to use "Client" instead of "Server."

5. Include the .proto file for client code generation.

```
<ItemGroup>
  <Protobuf Include="Protos\ forecast.proto"
  GrpcServices="Client" />
</ItemGroup>
```

6. Use the generated client classes to make a call to the gRPC service.

```
using System;
using System.Threading.Tasks;
using Grpc.Net.Client;
using Konstrukt.CalculationEngine.Grpc.Client.Protos;

class Program
{
    static async Task Main(string[] args)
    {
        var channel = GrpcChannel.ForAddress("https://
        localhost:{port for server}");
        var client = new BudgetForecast.BudgetForecast
        Client(channel);

        var request = new BudgetForecastRequest
        {
            HistoricalYears = { 2021, 2022 },
            Variables = { new Variable { Name =
```

```
"Inflation", Value = 2.5 } }
    };

    var response = await client.CalculateBudget
                    ForecastAsync(request);

    foreach (var forecast in response.Forecasts)
    {
        Console.WriteLine($"Year: {forecast.Year},
        Predicted Budget: {forecast.
        PredictedBudget}");
    }
  }
}
```

Running the Server and Client

With both the server and the client configured, we can test the server
and client. You can either run the projects using separate Visual Studio
instances, or configure multiple startup projects. If you do the latter, make
sure to add a Console.ReadKey(). If you do the former, run the server first,
then the client, and observe the output.

I've worked at two startups where we chose gRPC services over a
REST API to improve performance and scalability. The low latency,
high throughput, and strongly typed contracts made gRPC a compelling
solution. However, adopting gRPC had a steep learning curve, and we
spent considerable time figuring out the initial setup and debugging.
As with any migration, upgrade, or replacement, it's worth having a
discussion where the pros and cons are weighed.

Summary

In this chapter, we tackled the final steps of our migration process. We successfully migrated the remaining controllers and removed the YARP reverse proxy, streamlining our project. The old Konstrukt.SL.Main project and its dependencies were removed, leaving us with a cleaner solution.

We then focused on a few exciting new features, such as Minimal APIs, refactoring our controllers for a more streamlined approach. We took a look at other features such as ILogger, using a third-party logger provider, enabling AOT, and gRPC Minimal APIs offer a lightweight way to define endpoints directly in the Program.cs file, a high-performance framework for remote procedure calls.

Next up, we'll take a look at Konstrukt's Continuous Integration (CI) and Continuous Deployment pipeline (CD).

CHAPTER 8

Upgrading the Deployment Pipeline

We learned many lessons when we migrated to ASP.NET Core, and one of them was that you might have to make significant changes to your deployment pipeline. If you have a mixed solution, it can get tricky, depending on how the pipeline is set up. In this chapter, I want to highlight some changes and challenges that we had.

This chapter is not a guide on how to set up a continuous integration and deployment pipeline. There are many ways to do that and a variety of tools and services to choose between. But one thing I'm sure of is that you will need to change your pipeline when you migrate. And if you have a mixed solution, like we do, you will have additional challenges that you need to solve. In my experience the time and effort that goes into setting up and patching a pipeline is often forgotten when a team is estimating time and effort for migrations. And it can be a lot of work, particularly if you are not prepared. I hope that this chapter will give you some pointers to what sort of challenges you can come across and hopefully some solutions as well.

© Iris Classon 2024
I. Classon, *Migrating ASP.NET Microservices to ASP.NET Core 8*,
https://doi.org/10.1007/979-8-8688-1026-8_8

Konstrukt CI and CD Pipeline

When I first set up our pipeline, we were hosting all our services in Azure.
We were using something called cloud services for our web services,
and virtual machines tied together under a virtual IP. Cloud services in
Azure were an early PaaS offering that managed virtual machines, scaling,
and reliability for deployed applications. Azure App Service and Azure
Virtual Machines largely replaced Azure Cloud Services. However, when
we moved to a local cloud provider, we changed the setup, but we kept
the pipeline – including the tools and steps. The pipeline works like this
(Figure 8-1).

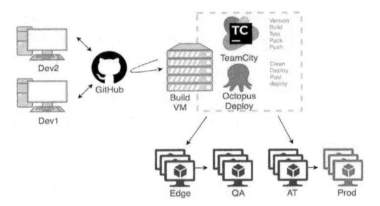

Figure 8-1. *Konstrukt CI/CD Pipeline*

The source code is hosted on GitHub (several repositories), and we
use Git for our version control. Our development branch is our master
branch, and we branch out releases in two-week cycles. For major patches
and features, we use temporary branches, but we try to avoid unnecessary
branching. Each developer works on their own local copy, committing
and pushing changes frequently to the remote repository. Our build
machine uses a build service called TeamCity, and the build service listens
for changes in the repository. When a commit has been made, it pulls
the latest version and goes through a series of build configurations, each

configuration containing several steps. A build agent is what executes a build configuration, and we have several agents that run in parallel. The diagram (Figure 8-2) shows the build steps in our pipeline.

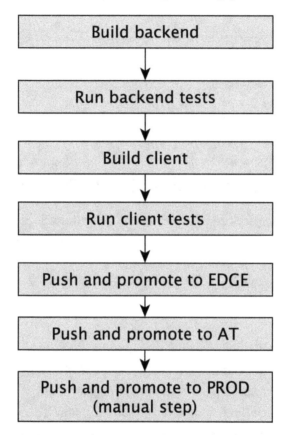

Figure 8-2. Konstrukt build steps

I won't go into the details of the configurations, but this is the process. Our solution is built and run as three separate parts: the client, the web API services, and tools. They all go through the following configurations, and the next configuration is only run if the previous one was successful.

Create Version

We use the build service to set the version number. If the commit was made on a release branch, the version is attached to the end of the version number. This is later parsed and used when we deploy the packages.

Build and Pack

In this step packages are restored, projects are built, and the deployment packages are created (NuGet packages).

Run Unit Tests and Run Integration Tests

The two test types are run as separate configurations as the integration tests rely on a physical database. We have scripts that run nightly to create backups and new test databases with real data.

Push

Since we deploy all our services at the same time, we need to sync packages, as front-end and back-end services are created by different agents. Therefore, in the final step, we make sure that everything was successful and that all the packages created are for the same version. The packages are then pushed to our NuGet server and deployed to either the EDGE server NuGet server or AT (acceptance testing server) – depending on whether this is a release or not.

Deployment Flow

Once the previous steps are finished, Octopus Deploy takes over. Octopus Deploy is our deployment service that manages the deployment to the various environments.

When a package is deployed to the EDGE environment successfully and we can ping all the services, the same packages are then deployed to the QA (quality assurance) environment for manual testing (done by both developers and our testers). Once everything is tested, a release is created by branching out a release branch; the packages are tested in the AT (acceptance testing) environment by testers and early adopters, before being released to production (PROD environment).

The deployment itself of the services is fairly straightforward. After some cleanup, we deploy the services as IIS web services, with just some minor differences for the ASP.NET Core services.

Pipeline Modifications

As I've mentioned before, we've had to make a few changes to our pipeline. The modifications you'll need to make depend on your current setup – and you might end up changing it a few times like we did. When we first started migrating some of the services, we decided to separate the projects by using a separate solution file. Solution files are generally used to group projects that are related, usually to simplify development (you can open related projects in the same Visual Studio instance) and deployment (you can run commands such as build on solution level). Our CI/CD setup before the migration was dependent on the solution file, and we were making use of the built-in steps for restoring packages and building a solution by adding a path to the solution itself. Out of the box, it works really well, until you add .NET Core and .NET Standard projects to the mix.

Three Options

We had three ways we could deal with this. The first one would be to add a second solution file for .NET Core and .NET Standard projects and create separate steps for restoring and building. The second one would be to have everything in one solution file, but change the existing steps to use command-line tools instead of plugins or TeamCity features. The third way would be to drop the solution file and script everything as in the second option. Unfortunately, our system is still somewhat of a distributed monolith, and therefore the third option isn't an option for us (yet). We decided on multiple solution files.

CLI First

.NET Core has a command-line-first approach, with excellent CLI tooling. TeamCity recommends that you use their .NET Core plugin for restoring packages and building and creating deployment packages. At the time the plugin had several issues, one of them was that it didn't support wildcard selection of multiple projects for restoring packages and building the assemblies. Adding a separate step for each build would be a pain to maintain, and it didn't work with mixed projects in a solution if you targeted the solution file. This is not a problem anymore. However, with separate solution files, we could run the restore or build command targeting Konstrukt.Core.sln. Moving forward we started consolidating the steps and moved away from built-in features and favored scripting the steps instead (by using native CLI tools instead of plugins). At Greenbyte, a different startup I worked at, we made the move to GitHub Actions. GitHub Actions is an automation tool integrated in GitHub that allows you to build, test, and deploy your code directly from GitHub. It offers seamless integration with repositories, enabling you to create workflows using YAML files that define the steps and conditions under which your code is built and deployed. We wanted to transition from TeamCity to GitHub Actions as we wanted to move from TeamCity's more GUI-driven configuration to GitHub's YAML-based workflow definitions. While TeamCity does support scripting and allows for sophisticated customization, GitHub Actions offered the advantage of being tightly integrated with our existing GitHub workflow and didn't require additional build servers that would need to be maintained. It started as a cost-saving effort, but in the end we really liked scripting our pipeline and being able to check in the pipeline using source control.

Running Tests

All our tests (for the back end) use NUnit, and we initially relied on the NUnit Console Runner. However, we encountered some issues when ASP. NET Core was relatively new. Fortunately, we soon transitioned to using the .NET CLI with the dotnet test command.

dotnet test is a powerful command-line tool for running tests in .NET projects. It offers many options to customize the test execution process. For example, you could run the following command:

```
dotnet test path/to/YourTestProject.csproj --configuration
Release --no-build --logger "trx;LogFileName=TestResults.trx"
--configuration Release: Uses the Release build configuration,
which is ideal for production-ready testing.
--no-build: Skips the build step if the project is already
built, saving time.
--logger "trx;LogFileName=TestResults.trx": Outputs test
results in TRX format, which can be useful for further analysis
or integration with other tools.
```

Some other common arguments are:

```
--filter: Allows you to run specific tests by name or category.
--collect "Code Coverage": Generates a code coverage report.
--results-directory: Specifies the directory where the test
results should be placed.
--verbosity: Sets the level of detail in the output, such as
minimal, normal, or detailed.
```

There are other arguments and I recommend taking a look at the documentation for the tool:

`https://learn.microsoft.com/en-us/dotnet/core/tools/dotnet-test`

The takeaway is that you will most likely need to maintain separate steps for different testing configurations. The easiest way to consolidate similar steps is by scripting them instead of relying on plugins and built-in features. While this depends on the build service you use, I've generally found that GUI-driven tools and services are slower to adopt changes and can be quite limiting. I cannot stress enough how much smoother our pipeline process became as we increasingly adopted scripting our build steps and using CLI tooling instead of relying on third-party plugins.

Deploying

Deploying required the least amount of work for us. We decided on not creating self-contained packages as we don't need to run multiple versions side by side, and we would rather keep the deployment packages small. We could also have used Docker containers. Docker is a platform that enables developers to package applications and their dependencies into lightweight, portable containers. A container is an isolated environment that includes everything needed to run an application: the code, runtime, system tools, libraries, and settings. Unlike virtual machines, containers share the host system's OS kernel but still run in complete isolation, making them more efficient and faster to start. Containerizing ASP. NET Core applications with tools like Docker simplifies deployments by packaging the app and its dependencies into a consistent environment. This reduces issues like "it works on my machine" and makes deployments more reliable across different platforms, whether on Linux or Windows. Transitioning to Docker requires changes in your CI/CD pipeline, such as building, testing, and deploying Docker containers instead of traditional packages.

We are also using IIS for our services and will continue to do so until we deploy to a different operating system. The changes we had to make included ensuring that we had the appropriate version of the .NET Core Hosting Bundle installed. The Hosting Bundle is required to host ASP. NET Core applications on IIS, and different versions of ASP.NET Core need specific versions of this bundle. Additionally, we had to set the .NET CLR version to "No Managed Code." This configuration is necessary because ASP.NET Core applications run in a separate .NET Core process rather than within the traditional .NET Framework's CLR (Common Language Runtime). By setting the CLR version to "No Managed Code," we ensure that IIS does not attempt to run the ASP.NET Core application using the .NET Framework's CLR, which would result in compatibility issues. We created two separate templates in Octopus Deploy, one for our "old" services and one for ASP.NET Core services. If you deploy self-contained packages and use the in-process hosting model on older Windows machines, you might need to disable the app pool for 32-bit (x86) processes. Don't forget to make sure that the identity used for the process has the required permissions. We have a separate account for all our deployment services and have set up our deployment steps in Octopus Deploy to use that identity. As we continued to refine our deployment strategy, we eventually decided to move from IIS on Windows to deploying on Linux machines. This transition was driven by the need to reduce infrastructure costs, as Linux servers often provide a more cost-effective solution. Additionally, Linux's native support for ASP.NET Core makes it an appealing choice for hosting these applications.

However, the switch to Linux did come with a learning curve, especially for our team, which was primarily accustomed to Windows environments. We had to familiarize ourselves with Linux commands, file structures, and system management. Despite this initial challenge, the long-term benefits, including cost savings and more straightforward configuration management, made the transition worthwhile.

Summary

One of the lessons we learned the hard way is that you can spend a significant amount of time adjusting the pipeline for a mixed deployment or a new deployment pipeline. The amount of time required depends on several factors, such as the flexibility of the tools and services you use, the size of the solution, and rigidness of the setup, among other things. Keep this in mind as you prepare a migration and adjust the pipeline as soon as you have something that builds so you can run your build process early on to avoid the common "it builds on my machine" problem, not to mention the disappointing surprise that you might have to spend a fair bit of time fixing a broken pipe.

CHAPTER 9

Navigating ASP.NET Core Upgrades

We've covered the steps for migrating from ASP.NET Framework to ASP. NET Core, and it seems appropriate to dedicate a section for upgrading to newer versions of ASP.NET Core. Depending on your experience, this might feel like a daunting task, with the fear of breaking changes. However, Microsoft has done a terrific job keeping their documentation up to date in terms of breaking changes. This chapter is here to guide you through each step, making the transition as smooth as possible. Whether you're moving from ASP.NET Core 2.x to 3.x, or taking the leap to the latest 8.x release, I've got you covered. If you are upgrading from one version to another, especially if you are skipping intermediate versions (e.g., moving from version 2 directly to version 7), I highly recommend that you thoroughly review all the upgrade sections for each intermediate version. Additionally, I recommend that you follow the upgrade from 2.X to 3.0 as a first step as it has the most significant changes.

Upgrading to ASP.NET Core 3.0

If your solution used global.json, update the version property to 3.0. Likewise update the target framework in the project file.

© Iris Classon 2024
I. Classon, *Migrating ASP.NET Microservices to ASP.NET Core 8*,
https://doi.org/10.1007/979-8-8688-1026-8_9

The global.json file is used to define the .NET SDK version that a project should use. Updating the version property to 3.0 ensures that the project is built with the correct SDK version, avoiding potential compatibility issues that might arise if multiple SDK versions are installed. Similarly, updating the target framework in the project file ensures the application takes advantage of new features, performance improvements, and API changes introduced in the updated version of ASP.NET Core. It is important to align both the SDK and target framework to prevent mismatches in build and runtime environments.

You can also remove the following package references from the project file as these packages aren't being produced for 3.X:

```
<ItemGroup>
  <PackageReference Include="Microsoft.AspNetCore.App"/>
  <PackageReference Include="Microsoft.AspNetCore.Razor.
  Design" Version="2.2.0" PrivateAssets="All" />
</ItemGroup>
```

These package references, Microsoft.AspNetCore.App and Microsoft.AspNetCore.Razor.Design, are no longer needed in ASP.NET Core 3.0 and later because they have been integrated into the shared framework, which is part of the .NET Core SDK itself. This means the necessary assemblies are already included with the runtime, so you don't need to explicitly reference them in your project file. The Microsoft.AspNetCore.App package, for example, is automatically referenced by the SDK, simplifying project files and reducing the need for manual package management. Some assemblies that were included in the two packages are not included in the SDK and should therefore be added explicitly as package references, for example, Identity UI, SpaServices, EntityFramework Core, and more.

```
<Project Sdk="Microsoft.NET.Sdk.Web">
  <PropertyGroup>
    <TargetFramework>netcoreapp3.0</TargetFramework>
  </PropertyGroup>
...
```

Kestrel and Hosting Model

The generic host (Host.CreateDefaultBuilder) is now the default host for all types of applications, including web applications. Kestrel is configured by using the ConfigureWebHostDefaults() method on the Host.

Before ASP.NET Core 3.0, the hosting model used IWebHostBuilder:

```
public static IWebHostBuilder CreateWebHostBuilder(string[]
args) => WebHost.CreateDefaultBuilder(args)
.UseStartup<Startup>();
```

In ASP.NET Core 3.0, the generic host model became the default for all applications, and Kestrel is configured with the ConfigureWebHostDefaults method:

```
public static IHostBuilder CreateHostBuilder(string[] args) =>
    Host.CreateDefaultBuilder(args)
        .ConfigureWebHostDefaults(webBuilder =>
        {
            webBuilder.ConfigureKestrel(serverOptions =>
            {
                // Set properties and call methods on options
            })
            .UseStartup<Startup>();
        });
```

Kestrel can be customized by setting server options such as connection limits, request size, and more. Here's an example with some basic configuration:

```
webBuilder.ConfigureKestrel(serverOptions =>
{
    serverOptions.Limits.MaxConcurrentConnections = 100;
// Set max concurrent connections
    serverOptions.Limits.MaxRequestBodySize = 10 * 1024;
// Set max request body size to 10KB
    serverOptions.AddServerHeader = false; // Disable the
    "Server" header for security reasons
});
```

Kestrel supports request trailers, and several request trailer extensions have been added in 3.0. Request Trailers are a feature in HTTP/1.1 and HTTP/2 that allow additional headers to be sent after the body of the request.

ASP.NET Core 3.0 added the following RequestTrailerExtensions:

- GetDeclaredTrailers

- SupportsTrailers

- CheckTrailersAvailable

- GetTrailer

Routing and Startup

Endpoint Routing has been added, which unifies routing for MVC, Razor Pages, and SignalR. The routing is now done in the Configure method with the UseEndPoints method mentioned earlier in the book. If the app calls UseStaticFiles, place it before UseRouting. UseAuthentication and UseAuthorization should be after UseRouting, but before UseEndpoints.

Other changes Startup changes:

- Replace IHostingEnvironment with IWebHostEnvironment.

- Replace IApplicationLifetime with IHostApplicationLifetime.

- Replace EnvironmentName with Environments.

- Replace UseMVC (or UseSignalR) with UseRouting.

- Use dependency injection over IServiceProvider in middleware for resolving services.

Newtonsoft vs. System.Text.Json

As part of the improvements in ASP.NET Core 3.0, Newtonsoft.Json (Json. NET) was removed from the default ASP.NET Core shared framework. It was replaced with System.Text.Json, which is faster and more efficient, but lacks some of the more advanced features of Newtonsoft.Json. Here's a comparison:

Newtonsoft.Json

- Mature and feature-rich: Supports complex serialization scenarios like polymorphic serialization, custom converters, handling of loops, etc.

- Advanced JSON handling: Commonly used when you need to support advanced scenarios, or you're working on legacy applications that already rely on Json.NET.

System.Text.Json

- Faster and more efficient: Built for performance, and it is now the default JSON serializer in .NET Core applications.

- Minimal dependencies: Built directly into .NET Core, reducing the need for external dependencies.

- Limited advanced features: It lacks some of the advanced capabilities of Newtonsoft.Json, such as custom serialization attributes and polymorphic type handling.

If your application requires features like advanced polymorphic serialization, custom converters, or if you're working on a project that relies heavily on Newtonsoft.Json, it may be necessary to continue using Newtonsoft.Json. However, if your app's JSON needs are simple or if performance is critical, System.Text.Json should be your go-to choice.

Other Breaking Changes

To see a comprehensive list of breaking changes, refer to the following pages.

Complete list of breaking changes:

```
https://github.com/aspnet/Announcements/issues?page=1&q=is%3Ais
sue+is%3Aopen+label%3A%22Breaking+change%22+label%3A3.0.0
```

Breaking API changes in Antiforgery, CORS, Diagnostics, MVC, and Routing:

```
https://github.com/aspnet/Announcements/issues/387
```

Breaking changes across .NET Core, ASP.NET Core, and Entity Framework Core:

```
https://learn.microsoft.com/en-us/dotnet/core/
compatibility/2.2-3.0
```

Upgrading to ASP.NET Core 3.1

Migrating from ASP.NET Core 3.0 to 3.1 is generally straightforward because 3.1 is a Long-Term Support (LTS) release that builds upon the features and improvements introduced in 3.0. One significant change is the new handling of SameSite cookies due to updates in browser implementations, which impacts remote authentication scenarios like OpenID Connect and WS-Federation.

Make sure you test interactions across various browsers and apply browser sniffing to handle older browsers that do not support the new SameSite=None behavior.

Upgrading to ASP.NET Core 5.0

You may be curious about the absence of a section on ASP.NET Core 4, but that's because there is no version 4.0. The versioning jumped from 3.1 to 5.0 to align with the overall .NET 5 unification strategy. This was part of Microsoft's effort to consolidate the .NET ecosystem under a single platform, and ASP.NET Core 5.0 is now part of the unified .NET 5 platform, consolidating .NET Framework, .NET Core, and Xamarin into a single framework. There's a significant performance improvement across various components, and new features such as Web API Analysers, HTTO/2 support, JSON improvements in System.Text.Json, and more. .NET Core is not referred to as .NET Core anymore, just .NET 5.

Additionally, the documentation pages for breaking changes now differentiate between binary and source compatibility. Binary compatibility means that existing compiled binaries work with the new version without recompilation, while source compatibility means that existing source code compiles and works with the new version without modification. Here is a list over breaking changes in ASP.NET Core, including Blazor and Kestrel specific changes.

Quoted Numbers

Quoted numbers in JSON are now deserialized to numbers by default, instead of throwing an exception. While this change makes deserialization more permissive, it could potentially impact applications that previously relied on exceptions being thrown for quoted numbers during deserialization. For example, this will not throw an exception:

```
string json = "{\"Id\":\"123\"}";
var product = JsonSerializer.Deserialize<Product>(json);
Console.WriteLine($"Product ID: {product.Id}");
```

Routing Changes

Starting with ASP.NET Core 5.0, the resource for authorization in endpoint routing is now the HttpContext, instead of just the endpoint. This change allows easier access to both the endpoint and route data (RouteData).

To continue accessing the endpoint, call GetEndpoint on the HttpContext if your app utilizes the endpoint resource:

```
var endpoint = httpContext.GetEndpoint();
```

To revert to old behavior:

```
AppContext.SetSwitch(
    "Microsoft.AspNetCore.Authorization.
    SuppressUseHttpContextAsAuthorizationResource",
    isEnabled: true);
```

HttpClient Status Codes

HttpClient instances created by IHttpClientFactory log integer status codes by default. This ensures that the numeric HTTP status codes (like 200, 404, etc.) are logged for better visibility in monitoring and debugging.

Client Certificate Renegotiation

Client certificate renegotiation has been disabled by default for HttpSys. Renegotiation is often considered a security risk and can negatively impact performance. Disabling renegotiation improves both security and speed.

If you rely on client certificate renegotiation, you'll need to explicitly enable it in your configuration.

UrlRewrite

The UrlRewrite middleware now preserves query strings by default when rewriting URLs. Previously, query strings could be lost unless explicitly handled. This was a defect that now has been fixed. If you prefer that the query string is removed, use the following for the action element:

```
appendQueryString="false"
```

Blazor

In Blazor 5.0.1, a bug affecting route precedence has been corrected. Previously, routes with lower precedence (such as catch-all routes *{slug}) could match before more specific routes like /customer/{id}, leading to incorrect routing. The routing system now follows the same precedence logic as ASP.NET Core, prioritizing route segments first and using route length only to break ties.

You can however use the PreferExactMatches attribute on the <Router> component to ensure exact matches are prioritized over wildcard routes:

```
<Router AppAssembly="@typeof(Program).Assembly"
PreferExactMatches="true">
```

Blazor now trims insignificant whitespace during rendering, optimizing HTML output. However, this change may affect applications that rely on whitespace for formatting. Additionally, the RenderTreeFrame class has been updated, transitioning its previously readonly public fields to properties, which could impact rendering logic in certain scenarios.

Another important change in Blazor is that JSObjectReference and JSInProcessObjectReference have been made internal, requiring the use of public interfaces instead. This makes the JavaScript interop feature more consistent with other Blazor patterns. Example:

```
var jsObjectReference = await JSRuntime.InvokeAsync<IJSObject
Reference>(...);
```

Kestrel Changes

Configuration changes are now detected by default, and default supported TLS protocol versions have been updated to improve security and HTTP/2 disabled over TLS on incompatible Windows versions.

Obsolete Types

AzureAD.UI and AzureADB2C.UI APIs

In .NET 5, AzureAD authentication has shifted toward Microsoft.Identity. Web as the preferred library for managing authentication.

BinaryFormatter Serialization Methods

The use of BinaryFormatter for serialization is discouraged as it is considered insecure, and alternative serialization methods should be used. Consider using JsonSerializer or XmlSerializer.

Kestrel and IIS BadHttpRequestException

The change was made to consolidate duplicate types and unify behavior across server implementations. Instead, use Microsoft.AspNetCore.Server.Kestrel.BadHttpRequestException and Microsoft.AspNetCore.Server.IIS.BadHttpRequestException with Microsoft.AspNetCore.Http.BadHttpRequestException.

You can find the full list of breaking changes here:

```
https://learn.microsoft.com/en-us/dotnet/core/compatibility/5.0
#aspnet-core
```

Upgrading to ASP.NET Core 6.0

Upgrading to ASP.NET Core 6.0 brings a range of new features, performance improvements, and several breaking changes that we must consider. Here is a summary of some of the breaking changes. Please refer to the documentation for the full list, as well as the binary vs. source compatibility comparison.

Routing and Endpoint Handling

Endpoint names are no longer set automatically, which could affect routing and endpoint identification. This is a feature that was added in RC 6.1 but reverted.

```
app.MapGet("/foo", GetFoo);
// RC 6.1: EndpointName automatically set to "GetFoo"
// Now: No automatic EndpointName
```

Use WithName to manually assign endpoint name:

```
app.MapGet("/foo", GetFoo).WithName("GetFoo");
```

The HTTPS Redirection Middleware now throws exceptions if there are ambiguous HTTPS port configurations.

There is also a new app.Use overload. This can cause a compiler error if you never call the next middleware. To resolve the error, use app.Run instead of app.Use.

Before (generated compiler warning):

```
app.Use(async (context, next) =>
{
    await DoStuffAsync();
    // next() not called
});
```

Use app.Run instead, if the middleware doesn't call next():

```
app.Run(async (context) =>
{
    await DoStuffAsync ();
    // next() not called
});
```

Minimal APIs and Middleware

Minimal API renames in RC1 and RC2. Some APIs in the minimal hosting model have been renamed, mainly removing "minimal" and "action" from API names with further renaming in RC2. The Microsoft. AspNetCore.Builder.DelegateEndpointRouteBuilderExtensions class has been removed, and its methods were merged into the existing Microsoft. AspNetCore.Builder.EndpointRouteBuilderExtensions class.

Validation has been added for TryParse and BindAsync methods. In the absence of a valid method, ASP.NET Core will search for invalid methods and, if any are found, throw an exception during startup.

ASP.NET Core Behavior Changes

The ActionResult<T> now defaults to setting the status code to 200.

```
public ActionResult<Model> Get()
{
    Response.StatusCode = StatusCodes.Status202Accepted;
    return new Model();
}
// Old behaviour: generates a 202 status response code.
// New behaviour: generates a 200 OK response
```

MVC doesn't buffer IAsyncEnumerable types when using System. Text.Json anymore since System.Text.Json added support for streaming IAsyncEnumerable<T> types.

The PreserveCompilationContext is no longer configured by default, which might impact runtime compilation scenarios. The change improves performance and startup time and results in a smaller build. Use the PreservceCompilationContext to preserve the compilation context:

```
<PropertyGroup>
  <PreserveCompilationContext>true</PreserveCompilationContext>
</PropertyGroup>
```

HttpSys

ClientCertificate property doesn't trigger renegotiation for HttpSys. Apps that use delayed client-certificate negotiation should call GetClientCertific ateAsync(CancellationToken) to trigger renegotiation.

Nullable Reference Types

Changes in nullable reference type annotations may lead to new warnings or errors in code with nullable contexts. Previously incorrect (or missing) warnings have been fixed.

Obsolete or Removed APIs and Members

1. The AddDataAnnotationsValidation method has been made obsolete, and you should use the new extension method EditContextDataAnnotationsExtensions. EnableDataAnnotationsValidation. The return value is the only difference:

   ```
   EditContext AddDataAnnotationsValidation(this
   EditContext editContext) { ... }
   IDisposable EnableDataAnnotationsValidation(this
   EditContext editContext) { ... }
   ```

2. Microsoft.AspNetCore.Http.Connections.Negotiate Protocol.ParseResponse. Removed. Replace with:

   ```
   NegotiateProtocol.ParseResponse(ReadOnlySpan<Byte>
   ```

3. Microsoft.AspNetCore.SignalR. HubInvocationContext. Removed. Replace with:

   ```
   HubInvocationContext(HubCallerConte
   xt, IServiceProvider, Hub, MethodInfo,
   IReadOnlyList<Object>)
   ```

4. Microsoft.AspNetCore.Http.Features.
    IHttpBufferingFeature. Removed. Replace with:

    ```
    Microsoft.AspNetCore.Http.Features.
    IHttpResponseBodyFeature
    ```

5. Microsoft.AspNetCore.Http.Features.
    IHttpSendFileFeature. Removed. Replace with:

    ```
    Microsoft.AspNetCore.Http.Features.
    IHttpResponseBodyFeature
    ```

6. Microsoft.AspNetCore.StaticFiles.
    StaticFileResponseContext (argument-less
    constructor). Removed. Replace with:

    ```
    StaticFileResponseContext(HttpContext, IFileInfo)
    ```

7. Microsoft.AspNetCore.Mvc.Infrastructure.
    ObjectResultExecutor (argument-less constructor).
    Removed. Replace with:

    ```
    ObjectResultExecutor(OutputFormatterSelector,
    IHttpResponseStreamWriterFactory, ILoggerFactory,
    IOptions<MvcOptions>)
    ```

8. Microsoft.AspNetCore.Mvc.ModelBinding.
    Validation.ValidationVisitor.AllowShortCircuiting
    ValidationWhenNoValidatorsArePresent. Removed.

9. Microsoft.AspNetCore.Mvc.ViewFeatures.View
    ComponentResultExecutor. Removed. Replace with:

    ```
    ViewComponentResultExecutor(IOptions
    <MvcViewOptions>, ILoggerFactory, HtmlEncoder,
    IModelMetadataProvider, ITempDataDictionaryFactory,
    IHttpResponseStreamWriterFactory)
    ```

10. CompatibilityVersion. Obsoleted.

11. Types related to RazorEngine have been marked as obsolete as compatibility can't be guaranteed. These are the affected APIs:

Microsoft.AspNetCore.Mvc.Razor.Extensions.
InjectDirective.Register
Microsoft.AspNetCore.Mvc.Razor.Extensions.
ModelDirective.Register
Microsoft.AspNetCore.Mvc.Razor.Extensions.
PageDirective.Register
Microsoft.AspNetCore.Razor.Language.Extensions.
FunctionsDirective.Register
Microsoft.AspNetCore.Razor.Language.Extensions.
InheritsDirective.Register
Microsoft.AspNetCore.Razor.Language.Extensions.
SectionDirective.Register
Microsoft.AspNetCore.Razor.Language.
IRazorEngineBuilder

You can find the full list of breaking changes here:

```
https://learn.microsoft.com/en-us/dotnet/core/compatibility/6.0
#aspnet-core
```

Upgrading to ASP.NET Core 7.0

Upgrading to ASP.NET Core 7.0 introduces fewer breaking changes compared to previous versions, but still includes several noteworthy improvements and updates.

Dependency Injection

API action methods now automatically resolve parameters from the DI container, simplifying controller methods. Example:

```
public ActionResult Post(MyCustomType service) => Ok();
```

As for SignalR, SignalR hub methods now also attempt to resolve parameters from DI, which could affect method signatures and how dependencies are injected. Example:

```
Services.AddScoped<SomeCustomType>();

class CustomHub : Hub
{
    // Old behaviour: type came from client
    // New behaviour: type resolved from DI
    public Task Method(string text, MyCustomType type)
    =>      Task.CompletedTask;
}
```

Configuration

Environment variables prefixed with ASPNET_ now take precedence: Environment variables with the ASPNET_ prefix now override other configurations, potentially impacting environment-specific settings.

Authentication

The AuthenticateAsync method behavior for remote authentication providers has changed. Instead of failing a call if there is no current user, the AuthenticateAsync now returns the following:

```
AuthenticateResult.NoResult()
```

In addition, .NET 7, ASP.NET Core introduces new authentication behavior. Previously, developers needed to explicitly set a default authentication scheme using AddAuthentication("MyD efaultScheme"). Now, when only one authentication scheme is registered, it is automatically treated as the default. For example, in the code AddAuthentication().AddOAuth("MyDefaultScheme"), "MyDefaultScheme" becomes the default scheme.

Logging

Log messages in Microsoft.AspNetCore.Mvc.Core now use different event IDs, instead of reusing IDs.

Endpoints

Endpoints configured with StaticFilesEndpointRouteBuilderExtensions. MapFallbackToFile only match HEAD and GET requests, in contrast to before when the endpoints matched to requests made with any request methods.

Also, The file-serving middleware will not pass a request to the next middleware if there's an active endpoint with a null request delegate.

Kestrel

The default HTTPS address and port bindings have been removed in Kestrel, requiring explicit configuration and Microsoft.AspNetCore.Server. Kestrel.Transport.Libuv and libuv.dll have been removed.

You can find the full list of breaking changes here:

```
https://learn.microsoft.com/en-us/dotnet/core/compatibility/7.0
#aspnet-core
```

Upgrading to ASP.NET Core 8.0

As you might have noticed, as new versions build upon the improvements made in previous iterations, we end up with fewer significant changes with each subsequent release. Here is the list for 8.0.

Antiforgery

For security reasons, IFormFile parameters in minimal APIs now require antiforgery checks. Although not recommended, you can opt out by using the following:

```
app.MapPost("/", (IFormFile formFile) => ...)
  .DisableAntiforgery();
```

JsonWebToken

The JwtBearer, WsFederation, and OpenIdConnect events now return a JsonWebToken by default instead of JwtSecurityToken, improving performance and adding async processing. The change isn't noticeable for most developers, unless you've down-casted to access claims or other reasons.

Obsolete or Removed Types and Methods

The ConcurrencyLimiterMiddleware has been marked obsolete as newer rate-limiting APIs have more functionality and better documentation. It is recommended that you use the newer rate-limiting middleware, for example, RateLimiterApplicationBuilderExtensions.UseRateLimiter. The rate-limiting middleware now also requires explicit configuration using AddRateLimiter. This is not allowed anymore and will throw:

```
Configure<RateLimiterOptions>(o => { })
```

Configure the rate limiter to avoid this:

```
Configure<RateLimiterOptions>(o => o
    .AddFixedWindowLimiter(policyName: "fixed", options =>
    {
        // configuration
    }));
```

ISystemClock has been marked obsolete and replaced with the TimeProvider abstraction, which offers more comprehensive time-related functionality for authentication and identity components.

Replace references to ISystemClock with TimeProvider in your codebase. For example:

```
var currentUtc = TimeProvider.GetUtcNow();
```

ASP.NET Core 8.0 replaces custom converters for ProblemDetails and ValidationProblemDetails with built-in System.Text.Json support. This may cause properties like Status to return null unless properly configured.

Configure JsonSerializerOptions with PropertyNameCaseInsensitive for proper serialization.

Minor Changes

The TrimMode setting for Web SDK projects now defaults to full.

The default ASP.NET Core port changed to 8080 in .NET containers.

You can find the full list of breaking changes here:

```
https://learn.microsoft.com/en-us/dotnet/core/compatibility/8.0
#aspnet-core
```

Summary

When you upgrade an ASP.NET Core project, you can expect a range of enhancements and performance improvements, but it's important to note that there may also be breaking changes. Each new version builds upon its predecessor by introducing more refined features and removing deprecated APIs. For instance, ASP.NET Core 3.x introduced Endpoint Routing and revamped the hosting model, while ASP.NET Core 5.0 focused on performance improvements and unification under the .NET 5 platform (and .NET Core was referred to as just .NET 5 from there on). ASP.NET Core 6.0 continued to enhance Blazor and middleware configurations while upgrading to ASP.NET Core 7.0 brought changes in dependency injection, authentication, and logging mechanisms. ASP.NET Core 8.0 included new antiforgery requirements, enhanced Blazor capabilities, and obsolescence of certain middleware components. In the next chapter, I'll share how to stay up-to-date with the latest developments in ASP. NET Core.

CHAPTER 10

Staying Up to Date

We migrated Konstrukt with enthusiasm and a certain degree of naivety. Future technical debt in our ASP.NET Core services wasn't on our mind back then, and we certainly spent little energy thinking about future maintenance. Shortly after the migration, a fresh release of ASP.NET Core emerged, and we were suddenly faced with a substantial amount of work if we wanted to maintain our up-to-date status. We lagged two versions when we did the second migration, and there were several breaking changes that had been announced well in advance – that we could have been prepared for.

A poorly planned migration can cause problems with technical debt in the future. This goes for all code we write, not only when we upgrade to newer versions. That being said, in my experience, the excitement and challenge of embracing change can sometimes cause us to overlook the necessity of planning. In the following pages, I would like to offer advice and provide resources that can help minimize technical debt in the future, ultimately making this journey a more seamless experience.

Framework Changes

I mentioned in one of the first chapters that one of the possible downsides of open source frameworks is that they frequently change – and breaking changes aren't unheard of. You probably use some team collaboration software to communicate with the team, and be that Slack or Teams (or other), I recommend that you set up alerts and notifications for the Core repositories.

© Iris Classon 2024
I. Classon, *Migrating ASP.NET Microservices to ASP.NET Core 8*,
https://doi.org/10.1007/979-8-8688-1026-8_10

Slack has a plugin that lets you easily subscribe to a repository, but there is always the option of using web hooks (custom callbacks to a URL based on a trigger). This is supported by most collaboration tools, including Microsoft Teams:

```
https://learn.microsoft.com/en-us/microsoftteams/platform/
webhooks-and-connectors/what-are-webhooks-and-connectors
```

And Slack:

```
https://github.com/integrations/slack
```

You can also subscribe to any repository and receive emails for all activity (Figure 10-1) or specific events by using the Custom option (Figure 10-2).

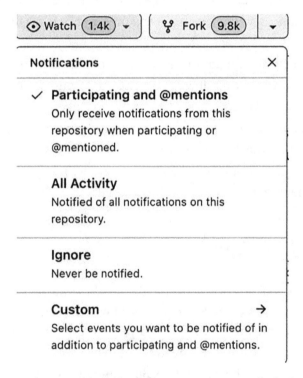

Figure 10-1. *You can subscribe to a repository on Github*

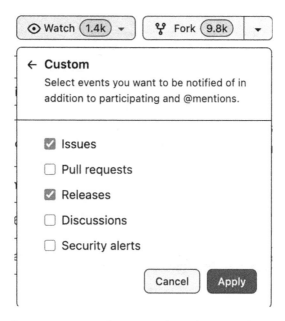

Figure 10-2. *Customize notifications by selecting the events you want to subscribe to*

The GitHub web hooks support a variety of triggers beyond those available in the dropdown menu:

`https://docs.github.com/en/webhooks`

You might also want to take a look at the support policy for the different versions of the framework if you're using an older version.

Announcements and Roadmaps

In the previous section, I mentioned subscribing to repositories, and the ASP.NET team has made it even easier for us to stay up to date by creating an announcement repository (Figure 10-3). If you subscribe to it, you will be notified on all issues and surrounding discussions. The issues have tags for "Announcement," "Breaching change," and the version numbers for easy searching.

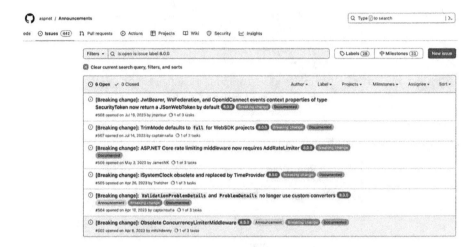

Figure 10-3. *You can use labels in your search to look for specific issues*

The aspnet/Announcements repository on GitHub is intended for announcements only, providing a centralized place to subscribe to updates and important notifications. On the other hand, the dotnet/aspnetcore repository is the main repository for the ASP.NET Core framework itself. It includes the source code, issues, discussions, pull requests, and other contributions related to ASP.NET Core. This repository is where the actual development and maintenance of the ASP.NET Core framework take place.

Documentation

Before I move on to the next piece of advice, I'd like to add a side note on documentation. Although the Microsoft documentation is sourced from different places, not just GitHub, you'll find a lot of the relevant documentation on GitHub.

You could in theory subscribe to the repository and be notified of changes – but bear in mind that not everything is going to be relevant, and it might instead create a lot of noise. You can find the documentation repository here: https://github.com/dotnet/AspNetCore.Docs

Align Architecture with New Conventions

Throughout the book, we've talked about conventions. Moving forward, I would recommend that you and your team try as much as possible to align your architecture with the new conventions that you decide to take on board. There are different ways to do this, but usually some sort of analyzer/linting tool can be helpful. There are numerous Roslyn Code Analyzers that integrate directly with the compiler. Roslyn Code Analyzers are powerful tools that integrate directly with the compiler to ensure your code adheres to specific conventions and best practices. These analyzers provide immediate feedback in the form of warnings or errors when your code deviates from the recommended guidelines. There are even specific analyzers for ASP.NET Core that can notify you if a controller returns an undeclared status code or undeclared success result and more. The package is reference like this and is typically added in the first PropertyGroup element:

```
<PropertyGroup>
  <IncludeOpenAPIAnalyzers>true</IncludeOpenAPIAnalyzers>
</PropertyGroup>
```

Testing

With test-friendly conventions such as dependency injection and modular architecture, ASP.NET Core is unit and integration test-friendly. One of the key packages for testing in ASP.NET Core is `Microsoft.AspNetCore.Mvc.Testing`. This package allows you to host the full web stack in memory while providing a test client. This approach includes database integration, removing the need to set up network or database environments for tests. This capability has been particularly beneficial, as it allows for end-to-end testing without the complexities of external dependencies.

This is the basic setup for creating integration tests with the Microsoft. AspNetCore.Mvc.Testing NuGet package:

1. Create a Test Project:
   Either create a new test project or use an existing one.
   Add a reference to the Microsoft.AspNetCore.Mvc. Testing NuGet package in the test project. You can do this by running the following command in the test project's directory:

   ```
   dotnet add package Microsoft.AspNetCore.Mvc.Testing
   ```

2. Add a Project Reference:
   In your test project, add a project reference to your ASP.NET Core project. This allows your test project to access the ASP.NET Core project's code.
   You can add a reference using the following command:

   ```
   dotnet add reference ../path-to-your-aspnetcore-project/YourAspNetCoreProject.csproj
   ```

3. Modify the ASP.NET Core Project File:
   In the ASP.NET Core project file
   (YourAspNetCoreProject.csproj), add the following
   lines to grant the test project access to internal
   members of the ASP.NET Core project:

```
<ItemGroup>
  <InternalsVisibleTo Include="TestProject" />
</ItemGroup>
```

   Replace "TestProject" with the name of your
   actual test project. This step ensures that the test
   project can access the Program.cs or other internal
   members of the ASP.NET Core project.

4. Create a Basic Integration Test:
   In the test project, create a new test class. For
   the purpose of this example, we will test the
   WeatherForecastController which is usually
   included in the basic ASP Core Web API template. It
   has a GET method that returns the weather forecast
   for five days.

```
using Microsoft.AspNetCore.Mvc.Testing;
namespace TestProject
{
    [TestClass]
    public class WeatherForecastIntegrationTests
    {
        private static WebApplicationFactory<Program>
        _factory;
        private HttpClient _client;

        [ClassInitialize]
```

```
public static void ClassInit(TestContext
context)
{
    _factory = new WebApplicationFactory<P
                    rogram>();
}

[TestInitialize]
public void TestInit()
{
    _client = _factory.CreateClient();
}

[TestMethod]
public async Task GetWeatherForecast_
ReturnsSuccess()
{
    // Arrange
    var url = "/WeatherForecast";

    // Act
    var response = await _client.GetAsync(url);

    // Assert
    response.EnsureSuccessStatusCode();
    Assert.AreEqual("application/json;
    charset=utf-8", response.Content.Headers.
    ContentType.ToString());
}

[ClassCleanup]
public static void ClassCleanup()
{
    _factory.Dispose();
```

```
        }
    }
}
```

This basic test sends a GET request to the /
WeatherForecast endpoint and checks that the
response is successful and that the content type is
correct.

5. Run the Tests:

    Execute your tests in the IDE or by using the dotnet
    test command:

    ```
    dotnet test
    ```

    The factory class **WebApplicationFactory<TEntr
    yPoint>** is part of the Microsoft.AspNetCore.Mvc.
    Testing package and is used to create a TestServer
    with the full application pipeline configured. This is
    useful for integration tests that need to interact with
    the full ASP.NET Core application stack.

    In addition, there is also a DefaultHttpContext
    object that can be mocked or instantiated directly in
    tests. In addition, there is also a DefaultHttpContext
    object that can be mocked or instantiated
    directly in tests. As mentioned earlier in the
    book, we discussed the importance of abstracting
    HttpContext away to reduce dependencies and
    make testing easier. However, in scenarios where
    you do need to interact with HttpContext directly
    in your tests, DefaultHttpContext provides a
    convenient way to simulate an HTTP context.

Community Resources and Tools

.NET Core is command-line oriented which has made it easier for the community to create tooling that fits with the .NET Core SDK. Here are some of my favorite tools, and packages, that can make our life easier. Some of them have been mentioned earlier in the book.

Dotnet Templates

You can find useful (and timesaving) dotnet templates at `https://dotnetnew.azurewebsites.net/`. I've used the NUnit test templates (before creating my own) and various ASP.NET Core SPA templates. It's not difficult to create your own templates, and they can be incredibly valuable, especially when working in a team where not everyone is comfortable starting from scratch. This documentation guides you through the few steps needed to create a custom template:

`https://docs.microsoft.com/en-us/dotnet/core/tutorials/create-custom-template`

Windows Compatibility Pack

If you need a shim for .NET Framework – only APIs so you can port code to a .NET Standard library and still be able to compile, you can use the NuGet package Windows Compatibility Pack. It provides a bridge by offering a subset of Windows-specific APIs, enabling you to compile and run your code with fewer changes. However, it's important to note that this package is intended as a temporary solution during migration. It doesn't guarantee full cross-platform compatibility, as some of the APIs might not be supported on non-Windows systems. You can find the library here:

`www.nuget.org/packages/Microsoft.Windows.Compatibility`

C# for Visual Studio Code

For C# editing support, lightweight development, and debugging tools for .NET Core, you can use the popular C# extension:

```
https://marketplace.visualstudio.com/items?itemName=ms-
vscode.csharp
```

Crowdsourced Tools and Frameworks

Thang Chung maintains a popular crowdsourced list of awesome tools and frameworks for .NET Core:

```
https://github.com/thangchung/awesome-dotnet-core
```

.NET Core Global Tools

.NET Core Global Tools, such as dotnet-ef and dotnet-portability-analyzer which we used earlier, are cross-platform console apps that can be installed globally on your machine. They can also be specific to a directory, or only run locally. You can find available tools on NuGet and even build your own.

You can search for dotnet tools on NuGet by filtering your search:

```
https://www.nuget.org/packages?packagetype=dotnettool
```

If you are interested in building your own .NET Core Global Tool, have a read here: `https://docs.microsoft.com/en-us/dotnet/core/tools/global-tools`

Stay Up to Date

At this point you might have noticed that a lot of the advice here is to combat the downsides listed early in the book. One of them was that it can get overwhelming for developers to stay up to date. Here are some additional resources for staying up to date.

Microsoft Blogs

Here is a small list of popular blogs:

- Web development: `https://blogs.msdn.microsoft.com/webdev/`

- Dotnet: `https://blogs.msdn.microsoft.com/dotnet/`

- Developer tools: `https://blogs.msdn.microsoft.com/developer-tools/`

Not official Microsoft blogs, but relevant nonetheless:

- Hanselman (mixed Microsoft content): `www.hanselman.com/blog/`

- Dotnet Foundation: `www.dotnetfoundation.org/blog`

Podcasts

- OnDotnet: `https://channel9.msdn.com/Shows/On-NET`

- The .NET Core Podcast (not Microsoft): `https://dotnetcore.show/`

Live StandUps

- ASP.NET Community StandUp: `https://live.asp.net/`

Twitter

- ASP.NET: `https://twitter.com/aspnet`

- .NET: `https://twitter.com/DotNet`

- .NET Foundation: `https://twitter.com/dotnetfdn`

Forums

- ASP.NET Forum: `https://forums.asp.net/`

Videos (General)

MS Build and Ignite videos are great resources. You can find them on Channel 9 under events: `https://channel9.msdn.com/Events/Build`

Video Training

If you want or need to do some technical training, you can find many official resources. Although there are many technical training providers, I would still recommend taking a look at what Microsoft has to offer first, as they are often a step ahead with new content. Besides the documentation, which contains tutorials for most frameworks and tools, there is Microsoft Learn – which among other things incorporates what used to be called Microsoft Virtual Academy. You'll find plenty of hands-on tutorials there and other resources.

Summary

Maintenance and technical debt are not easy topics. Being a startup, we struggled balancing new features for investors and clients with managing our growing system in such a way that we wouldn't accumulate technical debt faster than we could manage it. We kept our product in perpetual beta, which essentially means that the production version is always in an open beta and the clients participate in testing and giving feedback. Our developers were involved with support, first-, second-, and third-line support. We had biweekly architectural discussions and did full-day retrospectives after each sprint. Although we didn't do a lot of pair programming, we did have a rotating schedule for doing code reviews (alternating who is reviewing who). The daily standups helped us stay connected, even when some of us worked from home. However, these things alone are not enough.

The work you put in before accumulating the debt matters a lot. Therefore, when you're doing a migration, use the opportunity to embrace a more flexible and maintainable architecture as the one modern .NET promotes, stay up to date and engaged, test thoroughly, and use the available tools and resources. Best of luck and have fun!

Index

A

Acceptance testing (AT), 8, 23, 158
AccessController, 129
AddControllers(), 104
AddSwaggerGen(), 104
app.UseSwagger(), 104
ASP.NET Core, 187
  announcements and roadmaps,
    189, 190
  API features, 4
  architecture with new
    conventions, 191
  built-in DI, 5, 6
  container, 7
  cross-platform compatibility, 2
  cross-platform support, 8, 9
  documentation, 190, 191
  downside, 9
  history, 1, 2
  migration benefits, 4
  modularity, 6, 7
  open source and community
    driven, 8
  performance, 4, 5
  testing, 192–195
  web development evolution, 3
ASP.NET Core Blazor, 2

ASP.NET Core HttpContext
  abstraction interface
    creation, 114
  HttpContext.Current, 113
  implementation,
    IHttpContextAccessor,
    114, 115
  legacy system, 114
  register implementations,
    116, 117
  update dependent classes, 115
ASP.NET Core Identity
  comparison, Identity tables,
    124, 125
  hashed, 124
  migration to new
    schema, 125–127
ASP.NET Core MemoryCache, 50
ASP.NET Core SignalR, 19
ASP.NET MVC, 1, 2, 43
ASP.NET service to ASP.NET Core
  configuration providers
    command-line
      arguments, 107
    configuration API, 108
    file-based sources, 107
    IConfiguration interface, 108

GPSR Compliance
The European Union's (EU) General Product Safety Regulation (GPSR) is a set
of rules that requires consumer products to be safe and our obligations to
ensure this.

If you have any concerns about our products, you can contact us on

ProductSafety@springernature.com

In case Publisher is established outside the EU, the EU authorized
representative is:

Springer Nature Customer Service Center GmbH
Europaplatz 3
69115 Heidelberg, Germany